Railroad 1869
Along the Historic Union Pacific
Through Nebraska

Books by
Eugene Arundel Miller

Soldiers' Letters Home, A Family's Saga 1863-1919
    ISBN 978-0-9728511-2-1.

Railroad 1896, Along the Historic Union Pacific
    ISBN 978-0-9728511-3-8.

A Traveler's Guide to Railroad 1869
    ISBN 978-0-9728511-4-5.

Photographer of the Early West, The Story of Arundel Hull;
    ISBN 978-0-9728511-0-7.

Arundel C. Hull, Ghost Photographer for
    William H. Jackson ISBN 978-0-9728511-1-4.

Railroad 1869, Along the Historic Union Pacific
    Through Nebraska. *ISBN 978-0-9728511-5-2.*

Railroad 1869, Along the Historic Union Pacific
    Across Wyoming. *ISBN 978-0-9728511-6-9.*

Railroad 1869, Along the Historic Union Pacific
    In Utah to Promontory. *ISBN 978-0-9728511-7-6.*

Railroad 1869, Along the Historic Union Pacific
    State-by-State *(Set)*
    ISBN 978-0-9728511-8-3.

Railroad 1869
Along the Historic Union Pacific
Through Nebraska

Eugene Arundel Miller

Antelope-Press
Mill Valley, California

Railroad 1869
Along the Historic Union Pacific
Through Nebraska

By Eugene Arundel Miller

Printed in the United States of America.......Copyright 2012

Cover: "Osceola" the locomotive derailed and wrecked at Plum Creek, was rebuilt in Council Bluffs and was back in service a few months later. Courtesy Union Pacific Railroad Museum.

Publisher's Cataloging-In-Publication Data
(Prepared by The Donohue Group, Inc.)

Miller, Eugene A. (Eugene Arundel)
Railroad 1869 : along the historic Union Pacific through
Nebraska / Eugene Arundel Miller.

   p. : ill., maps ; cm. -- (Railroad 1869 along the historic Union
Pacific state by state)

   Includes bibliographical references.
   ISBN: 978-0-9728511-5-2

   1. Union Pacific Railroad Company--History. 2. Railroads--
Nebraska--History--19th century. 3. Nebraska--History--19th
century. 4. Nebraska--Description and travel. I. Title. II. Title:
Railroad eighteen hundred and sixty-nine III. Title: Through
Nebraska

HE2791.U551 M55 2012
385/.09/782   2011963105.

Antelope-Press
410 Monte Vista Ave. Mill Valley, Ca. 94941

Dedication

This book is dedicated to my
wife, Phyllis Forsling Miller,
mother, Nina Hull Miller,
sister, Millicent Miller Sacio, and
editor extraordinaire, Vicki Weiland.

About the Author

Eugene Arundel Miller grew up in Lexington, Nebraska, the youngest grandson of Arundel C. Hull, one of the early photographers along the route of the new transcontinental railroad. After graduating from Colorado State University and Georgia Institute of Technology, Miller served in the post Korean War era first as a Navy Seabee, then Civil Engineer Corp officer. He lives and has practiced geotechnical engineering in the San Francisco Bay Area for forty-five years. He has written articles for various professional journals and magazines.

Miller's inheritance of Arundel Hull's historic photographs led to his research, writing, and publication of Hull's biography, then *"Railroad 1869"* and three other historical non-fiction books. including *"Soldiers' Letters Home".*

This book is one of three new volumes with which he has republished *"Railroad 1869",* one book for each state  the railroad crossed in its initial years. In addition to the text and photographs which were part of the original book each of the three new volumes includes an Appendix: A Traveler's Guide of what to see along the way and how to find it.

Preface

Occasionally during our childhood years my sister and I sat with our mother, Nina Hull Miller, to look at an album of her father's photographs. These were precious keepsakes, prints made from glass-plate negatives by her father, Arundel C. Hull, as he traveled the Union Pacific Railroad in the construction years of 1867, 1868, and 1869. During those three years he photographed many of the present-day towns when they were little more than a scattering of a few wooden-front buildings on a bleak expanse of western prairie.

During 2002 and 2004, retracing Hull's travels I traveled all of the 1,094 miles of the original Union Pacific Railroad from Omaha to the 1869 Golden Spike site at Promontory, Utah. My objective was to research local histories of the transcontinental railroad era and to photograph, if I could, the same sites captured in Hull's historic prints.

Finding the historic locations along the Union Pacific Railroad was fascinating and I realized that others might enjoy a similar experience.

Here, in *Railroad 1869 Along the Historic Union Pacific through Nebraska,* we will follow the Union Pacific Railroad westward from its faltering start in Omaha, meet some of the "money men," help right the derailed train at Plum Creek, meet the legendary bad man Jack Morrow, and venture down several dangerous main streets in the new wide-open towns.

In this book and in companion books for Wyoming and Utah, we have included numerous vignettes of local history from those dramatic times, excerpts from the diary of Arthur Ferguson, a young railroad surveyor, and news items from *The Frontier Index,* the newspaper-on-wheels. Historic photographs by Arundel Hull and others including John C. Carbutt, Andrew J. Russell, J. B. Silvis, and William H. Jackson, help tell the story.

In each of our three books we have included an Appendix with maps and driving directions for what to see and how to find it in those states.

Eugene Arundel Miller 2012

Original painting by Francis Campbell. Used with permission.

Contents

Railroad 1869 through Nebraska

Photograph by Carbutt. Courtesy Union Pacific Railroad Museum.
The Track laying crew taking a brief rest.

Introduction

In the early 1800s the young American nation struggled to define itself: its government, its economy, its identity. As the country's frontier crossed the Ohio River, eyes turned farther west. The vast open lands between the populated east and the Pacific Ocean seemed an insurmountable barrier to trade and expansion.

Asa Whitney, an obscure New England merchant foresaw a trade link connecting the eastern half of America with its West Coast and the Pacific. Inspired, Whitney wrote up a plan of action - "A Railroad from Lake Michigan to the Pacific" to be built privately with government incentives: grants and government backed bonds.

Asa Whitney's vision became reality when the Pacific Railway Act became law in 1862. Government land grants and government backed bonds emerged as the great inducements for private investment. However, government decisions were stalled by Congressional disagreements.

When the Civil War removed the Southerners from the Congressional debate, the promoters got busy, ready to seize a great "entrepreneurial opportunity." The newly formed Union Pacific Railroad won entitlement to build westward from the Missouri River. In California the "Big Four," Huntington, Hopkins, Crocker, and Stanford, formed the Central Pacific Railroad with their own capital and received government approval to build eastward from Sacramento. When construction started in 1864, the two railroads were a "whole country apart." But during the following four years, as their respective rails drew closer, an increasingly intense race developed. The government had not clearly determined the railroad meeting point and each company raced to construct as many miles of track as possible to reap the benefits of land grants and government backed bonds.

Investors could readily see that a completed railroad across the country would hasten settlement of the western lands and that railroad companies could monopolistically control rates for freight and passengers. The early Union Pacific officials had an even greater view. They pontificated "The profit is not in operating the railroad but in BUILDING it!" The entire enterprise thus attracted dreamers, schemers, and influence peddlers, giving rise to all manner of skimming, side deals, and corner cutting.

In this Nebraska book we follow the Union Pacific Railroad from Omaha westward during the first three years of construction. We track the Union Pacific as it struggles to build the first few miles out of Omaha, then picks up speed as it becomes better organized in Columbus. We follow the surveyors and construction crews as they run into trouble with displaced Native Americans (known then as Indians), from Grand Island westward. And then we shudder at the lawlessness in the new towns of Ogallala, Julesburg, and Sidney.

Later, in subsequent volumes, we shiver during the most severe winter weather in decades, then swelter as the workers tame the great Wyoming desert and blast their way down the steep hard rock canyons of Utah. Finally, we enjoy the celebration and libations during the grand "finale," driving the Golden Spike at Promontory.

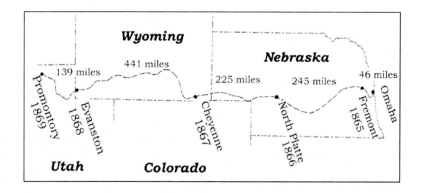

Union Pacific Railroad.
Construction Progress 1864-1869.
From Omaha, Nebraska west to Promontory, Utah.

Thousands of people contributed their brains and brawn to the construction effort. The most visible workers were doggedly determined construction crews. But there were invisible thousands who contributed: surveyors working miles ahead of the constructors, woodsmen and sawmill operators laboring in forests far out of sight, and hundreds of workers back east who produced the rails, switches, fish plates, and spikes, work clothes and shoes, shovels and picks. Crews in Chicago were precutting timbers, making columns, braces, and beams ready to ship out on the line for bridges. There were teamsters, bull whackers, graders, and spikers, the cowboys, butchers and cooks who provided fresh meat and fed the work crews, well diggers, water tank and windmill builders, and miners searching for coal to fuel the locomotives. Not to be forgotten are the newly recruited train crews, telegraphers, stations masters, rail maintenance crews, machinists, boiler makers, pipe fitters, and carpenters.

Disdained by some but celebrated by others were the whiskey purveyors, saloon operators, dance-hall owners and girls, and the much needed legitimate merchants. All of them were seeking opportunity, excitement, and riches.

Railroads created thousands of new jobs and brought thousands of new inhabitants to the West. The entire nation was changed in ways that could not have been imagined. During the next century these first 1,094 miles of the Union Pacific Railroad grew into a nationwide transportation system.

Union Pacific Directors.
Standing: Herb Hoxie, Samuel Reed.
Seated: Silas Seymour, Sidney Dillon, "Doc" Durant, John Duff.

Among the thousands of individuals who contributed their energies and efforts in creating the monumental transcontinental railroad, many characters emerged "larger than life" for their roles in the construction effort. Among the giants were these railroaders:

Oakes Ames (pictured) and his brother Oliver earned their initial fortune manufacturing picks and shovels for gold miners. They invested their wealth in the UPRR and took their credit up to the limit to help finance the railroad construction.

Oliver, a tactful manager and careful bookkeeper, became President of the railroad during the hectic years of 1866-1871.

Thomas C. ("Doc") Durant, the railroad's Vice President and General Manager, worked at almost every level of the construction effort. He was a persistent lobbyist and constantly interfered with the work of more competent men under him. He "didn't stop at trifles . . . ." He organized the "Great Excursion," a junket to show influential government officials, financial backers, and reporters a glowing picture of construction progress and the great opportunities it created. As President of Credit Mobilier, which was the financial conduit for much of the diverted funds, he was widely accused of bribery, fraud, and scandal during construction and in the following years.

Grenville M. Dodge, trained as a Civil Engineer, and as a General he directed reconstruction of many Southern railroads for the Union Army. At the end of the war, Dodge was recruited to be the UPRR Chief Engineer. He agreed, but with the proviso that, "I must have absolute control in the field." Later, as construction moved across Wyoming, he grew increasingly less tolerant of Doc Durant's interference, ill-advised policies, and extravagant squandering of limited funds. After a showdown meeting with Durant in 1868 at Fort Sanders, Wyoming, Dodge was confirmed as being in complete charge of the construction effort.

Silas Seymour, the "Colonel" and Chief Consulting Engineer, had no official authority over the construction forces but he injected himself in many field decisions as Durant's representative. Seymour's insistence on a route change in Wyoming precipitated a showdown meeting of officials during which Durant and the "Colonel" were resoundingly overruled, but it slowed him only slightly. Soon after, Durant reportedly designed the terrifying Dale Creek Bridge which had to be replaced after only eight years.

Samuel Reed's initial job as the surveyor was to locate the railroad route across Wyoming and Utah. Despite Durant's repeated interference, construction advanced westward, and Reed became Chief of Construction, in charge of all grading, track laying, bridges, and numerous tunnels.

John Casement and his brother Dan were hard-bitten and fearless bosses who took firm command of the construction. Both of the Casement brothers had been Union Officers and both men were unusually short: Jack was 5' 4", Dan, "five feet nothing." After General Dodge brought them on board, they drove the roughest of Irish crews to grade most of the route and lay the track west of Fremont.

Railroad 1869 through Nebraska

*I*mportant to our historical travelogue are other lesser known individuals who added to the record of the railroad's monumental effort and its effects:

Arthur N. Ferguson, a young man from Bellevue, Nebraska, signed on as a surveyor's rod man in the railroad's "corps of engineers." His diaries survived the years and describe his adventures as part of a location survey crew in Nebraska and into Wyoming during 1865 and 1866. He and his crew worked far in advance of the construction across Nebraska leaving a single line of stakes for the location of the tracks.

During the following three years Ferguson's crew marked lines and grades for excavations, embankments, and bridges. His journals are a treasure of first-hand observations about the untamed country and rigors of the work at the time. He describes the beauty of the vast terrain, wild weather, prairie fires, hunger, hostile Indians, his loneliness, and offers insightful observations about sweeping changes the completion of the railroad would have on our young and expanding nation.

Professor John C. Carbutt photographically recorded the UPRR's great promotional excursion to the 100th Meridian, where the arid west begins. Carbutt's widely distributed photographs and stereo cards of the trip did much to excite the nation about the railroad and the forthcoming link to the Pacific Ocean.

Leigh Freeman and Fred Freeman were a pair of unrepentant Southern sympathizers. They seized an opportunity to buy a dying local newspaper at Fort Kearny, Nebraska and created *The Frontier Index,* a newspaper-on-wheels. The Freemans and their newspaper moved westward, sometimes following, but often ahead of the railroad. Their outspoken and piously opinionated sheet gained notoriety across Nebraska and Wyoming. It came to an end in Bear River City, Wyoming, when it was burned out by a mob of infuriated railroad workers.

Arundel C. Hull. At 21 this young photographer could not resist the excitement and adventure offered by construction of the railroad. In the spring of 1867 he gathered together his photographic gear and started west from Omaha traveling from town to town. At each  stop he picked out interesting views he thought were saleable, made photographs with glass-plate negatives, and developed them on the spot. After making a few prints, he sold what he could and moved on. He traveled along the railroad across Nebraska and into Wyoming, then detoured to Colorado gold country. In the spring of 1868 he returned and followed the railroad crews across Wyoming. Lonesome and out of money, he returned to Omaha to work in the new Jackson Brothers Gallery. The following year Arundel Hull and William Jackson followed the UPRR through the Utah Canyons and out to Promontory Summit where the transcontinental railroad connection had just been completed.

And As in every era there are many colorful characters, such as:

John A. (Jack) Morrow.

The Morrow ranch and way-station lay near the confluence of the North and South Platte Rivers in western Nebraska. Morrow was widely known to charge outrageously high prices for supplies.

Also discomfiting were the frequent wagon train robberies in the vicinity widely alleged to be Morrow's doing.

Morrow continued his opportunism as he followed railroad construction crews across Wyoming, becoming a major supplier of ties. His name appears in stories carried by *The Frontier Index* and he appears in photographs taken by Arundel Hull.

A global location 100 degrees west of the Prime Meridian in England, the 100th Meridian was a major milestone 247 miles west of Omaha.

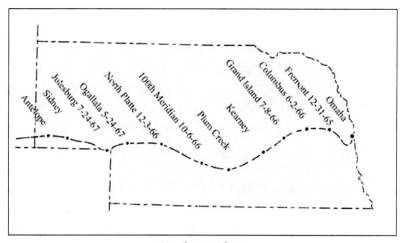

Nebraska
Union Pacific Railroad Construction 1864-1867.
From Omaha, Nebraska to Cheyenne, Wyoming.

1. Ground Breaking

In 1863 the investors in the newly organized Union Pacific Railroad maneuvered for their personal positions and set the stage for their momentous effort.

The Board of Directors elected General John Dix President and financier Thomas C. "Doc" Durant, Vice President and General Manager. Peter A. Dey, an experienced civil engineer, became Chief Engineer.[1] All three men had been involved in construction of a railroad across Iowa. Dey eschewed the personal maneuvering but saw his new appointment as "the best position in my profession..." Durant saw it as an opportunity to bolster his many private interests.

Railroad 1869 through Nebraska

Chief Engineer Dey surveyed four locations along the Missouri River as possible sites for a river crossing and a location for the Union Pacific's eastern terminal. He recommended that the terminus be at Bellevue, Nebraska. From there the rails could follow a uniform slope up the Elkhorn Valley, across the divide, and then follow the Platte Valley westward. His second choice for the terminal was Omaha. From Omaha, the route was directly west up a rather steep grade at first but the route was considerably shorter, an advantage for future railroad operations. Rivalries immediately erupted between the two towns. After Doc Durant took the report and recommendations to President Lincoln, "wealthier" Omaha was approved as the terminus. Many of the railroad "interests" had already bought up land in Omaha and directly across the river in Council Bluffs, Iowa. President Lincoln himself owned a quarter section of land in Iowa directly across the river from Omaha. On December 2, 1863, Doc Durant received the President's approval of the crossing location and telegraphed Dey to start construction at once. That very afternoon there was a groundbreaking ceremony with great ballyhoo at the foot of Omaha's Davenport Avenue. But it would be months before any actual track was laid.

With the initial route decided Engineer Dey proceeded to lay out the route from Omaha directly westward to the Elkhorn River. He estimated construction cost to be $20,000 to $30,000 per mile, but as work began, and against Dey's advice, Doc Durant raised it to $50,000 per mile. The profit-taking had begun.

Durant apparently decided he needed a more "compliant" engineer and early in 1864 appointed Col.

Silas Seymour his "Consulting Engineer." Seymour was immediately directed to re-survey the route and terminus, a duplication of Dey's work. That fall Seymour announced that the location should be changed.

The Oxbow Route

Instead of going west from Omaha the railroad was to go south around the Missouri River oxbow near Bellevue, through the low bluffs to Muddy Creek, west past Papillion, and then northwest to Elkhorn.

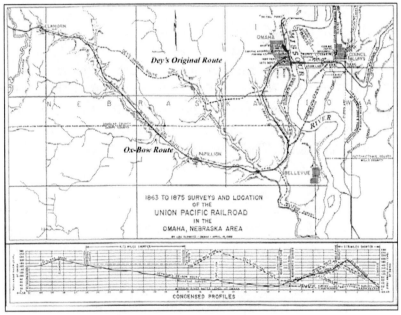

Courtesy Lou Schmitz.
Seymour's Circuitous "Oxbow Route."

Seymour's cost estimate was $28,000 per mile. The change would lengthen the line by nearly nine miles, ostensibly to eliminate "steep" grades; however, the

15

change merely shifted some of the unfavorable slopes to other locations.

The circuitous "oxbow" route provided more "early money," some nine extra miles with $16,000 per mile of extra government subsidy. More importantly, it also raised the speculative value of land in Bellevue. Doc Durant with his prior purchases of cheap land was poised to take advantage. After a long series of arguments and a flurry of reports, the government commissioners ruled the change could be made only if it eliminated the Elkhorn grade, which it did not.

Durant ignored the government decision and ordered construction to proceed along the oxbow route. He contracted with his cohort, Herbert M. Hoxie, to build the first 100 miles at the inflated price of $50,000 per mile. For those who knew the crafty Doc Durant the objective was clear .... to make big money on construction. "Only fools and dreamers can afford to wait around until actual traffic begins to pay its way."

Chief Engineer Dey was so incensed with Seymour and Durant for overruling his engineering decisions and their maneuvers for extracting early profit that he resigned.

Just five days later work stopped. Great controversy erupted and the question of the terminus location and route was reopened. As various competing inducements were offered to the railroad from community groups in Omaha and Papillion, the United States Government sent Lt. Col. James H. Simpson to review the matter and resolve it. Simpson arrived July 4, 1865.

The pressure on Durant was now enormous. The railroad was required to complete the first 40 miles of track by the end of 1864 in order to validate its entitlement. Time was running out. Within a week Durant ordered construction to restart and sent the construction crews down the oxbow route. He risked it all should Simpson's findings conflict with his choice, but his political influence and his cronies in Washington gave him considerable advantage. In September Lt. Col. Simpson filed his report and five days later the oxbow route was approved by President Andrew Jackson. Durant won the gamble. He and other insiders gained nearly a half million dollars and thousands of acres of land grants.[2]

Forty years later the Union Pacific Railroad relocated their main line from the circuitous oxbow route to the straight line "Lane Cut Off" directly west from the city of Omaha. The relocated route, just south of the present day Highway I-80, follows the route originally planned by the first engineer, Peter Dey.

Courtesy Union Pacific Railroad Museum.
Union Pacific's first locomotive "General Sherman."

Railroad 1869 through Nebraska

In the background during the early turmoil the middle level railroad officials were struggling to line up eastern suppliers and shippers, and to organize the first work crews. By the end of 1864 the inexperienced track crews had completed only 40 miles, but they reached Fremont, Nebraska and the railroad earned the first of the government subsidies.

It was a start, but the next thousand miles looked like a bewildering impossibility. Major changes were obviously needed. While the work forces wintered in Fremont the railroad induced General Grenville Dodge to organize and direct the construction work. Dodge approached it like a military campaign. In 1866 the reorganized crews completed rails across the 100th Meridian and reached milepost 290 at North Platte. At the end of 1867 the crews wintered in Cheyenne, Wyoming. It had taken three years to cross Nebraska, 516 miles.

!

Photograph by Arundel C. Hull.
Panorama of Omaha from Capitol Hill, 1868.

2. Omaha

With the resignation of experienced engineer Peter Day in 1865, important engineering decisions were left to dubious individuals. The overriding motivation seemed to be to buy materials and build the railroad at the absolute least cost, regardless of the government's construction specifications.

Colonel Seymour assumed widespread authority and was now directing construction. He initially ordered the use of relatively light rail (44 lbs. per yard)3 and instructed that the rails be laid on parallel timbers. That combination had been tried in the east and abandoned. It spelled potential disaster for the safe operation of trains and the proposal created a strong reaction from those more knowledgeable. Seymour backed off, and on July 10, 1865 the first wrought iron rail weighing 50 lbs. per yard, was laid on customary cross ties.[4]

Agonizingly Slow

When Seymour's oxbow route was finally selected, Herb Hoxie was awarded the contract for the first 100 miles. He sent untrained, poorly supervised crews out with little more than strong backs, shovels, wheelbarrows, and one-horse dump carts. With little or no direction the new crews leveled the grade, wrestled cross ties into place, and laboriously laid rails. The end of the line crept south toward Bellevue and around the oxbow. By November ties and rails had been laid to just beyond the sixteen-mile mark near Papillion, and Hoxie boasted that they were making a half mile per day.

The sixteen miles was hardly an outstanding accomplishment but by late October it was enough for a gala celebration to help raise more capital. Doc Durant journeyed all the way out from New York to preside at the celebration and to welcome popular General Tecumseh Sherman as the guest of honor. Guests from the east traveled, by steamer, up the Missouri River to the Omaha dock.

Waiting for them was the railroad's first locomotive, the "General Sherman," and two flatcars, fitted with overturned nail kegs as seats for the passengers. The celebration train lurched south on unevenly laid rails along Mud Creek, around "Seymour's Oxbow," and on to the end of track. At Sailing's Grove (near the present day 72nd Street) the party picnicked on roast duck and champagne. An Omaha newspaper reported that, "The party was jolly going out and hilarious coming in."

The crews resumed grading, placing ties, and stringing out rails with great urgency. Union Pacific had to build 40 miles by the end of the year to preserve the railroad's entitlements to land and bonds. Their goal was another 24 miles to reach Fremont.

Steamers and Ties

In spite of the Union Pacific's promotional bravado, the construction was slow and often a fumbling affair. Supply contracts were granted to eastern suppliers, but the rails, track fittings, and heavy equipment were slow to travel west. Materials could be transported from the east only part way by rail. At a railhead in Missouri freight had to be reloaded onto freight boats for a laborious two week trip up the river to the Omaha landing. The steamer portion of the journey was particularly unpredictable. The river was full of hazards: sand bars, shifting channels, and snags. The river boats could safely use the river for only about three months out of the year. In addition captains often demanded cash up front and some of them ignored their contracts with the railroad if a better paying cargo came along.

Faced with this transportation predicament Durant bought a steamboat and ordered two flat bottomed barges. The steamboat "Elk Horn" made its initial trip up the Missouri in only ten days, notably faster than the normal river traffic.5 The Union Pacific soon added other river boats, creating a fleet of six vessels plying the river.6 Now there was competition and other river boat captains became more cooperative.

Photograph by Carbutt. Courtesy Union Pacific Railroad Museum.
The Burnetizing Plant.
Cottonwood ties are placed in a tank and pressure saturated with a zinc solution, a slow laborious process.

Durant faced another predicament. Hardwood ties came from the forests in Minnesota and Wisconsin. They were costly and the delivery to landings along the river was unacceptably slow. Hoxie complained that his graders and track gangs ran through ties faster than they were being supplied. Wood cutters were sent to search for timber along the west side of the Missouri River. They found mainly soft cottonwood, but all things considered, the railroad had little choice but to use it. Durant ordered sawmills built at Omaha and upstream along the river. That winter the mills produced forty thousand ties ready to float down river in the spring. But even forty thousand ties were only sufficient for 15 or 20 miles of track. In their zeal to find tie timber the wood cutters cleared local forests of every usable tree.

Unfortunately, cottonwood had the "staying power of cardboard." It was good for two or three years of service at most.

But for Doc Durant's purpose that was long enough to pass inspections and get government approvals. When other Union Pacific Railroad officials pressured Durant for more durable ties, he tried a questionable new technique, "burnetizing." It involved pressure-saturating the cottonwood with a zinc solution.

A burnetizing plant was set up at Omaha. The plant could treat 500 ties per day, but six days production was enough for a mile of track. The burnetized ties were slightly more durable than un-treated wood. They were much heavier and nasty to handle. The process was not very effective, but work on the railroad could proceed.

During the summer and autumn of 1865 mountains of material piled up at Omaha. Ties, rails, and rail hardware were stockpiled along the river front. Locomotives, freight cars, and every other kind of material were delivered dockside as well.

In early 1866 ties and other construction supplies were reloaded onto rail cars and shipped west to a new supply depot at the end of the line, Fremont.

Herndon House

Doc Durant realized that the completion of 245 miles and crossing the 100th Meridian would be a great promotional opportunity. He invited a plethora of government officials, railroad commissioners, and other "influentials" on a Great Excursion to celebrate the event. At Omaha the celebration was to be centered at the Herndon House, Omaha's first hotel of consequence (named after President Lincoln's former law partner). However, the hotel was not ready for fine guests. It was somewhat seedy and in disarray from ten years of hard use.7 Moreover, its owner was in a series of skirmishes to kick out the old "host," or "manager" in favor of a Mrs. Brownson, who planned a renovation. One morning the old tenant arrived to find Mrs. Brownson's cook stove standing in the kitchen and his own stove heaved over the fence.8 The condition was so unsettled that most of the guests left.

Photograph by Arundel C. Hull.
International Hotel (formerly Herndon house), 1867.

Col. Seymour returned to Omaha from a trip to the end of track and saw that Durant's planned Great Excursion might well be derailed by the hotel problem so he waded into the matter with a heavy hand. He soon wired Durant, "The difficulties at the Herndon House were amicably arranged and Mrs. Brownson, the new lessee, was fully installed." The Col. observed that, "Mrs. Brownson will do much towards establishing the doctrine of social and business equality and vested rights of women, if she succeeds in the hazardous undertaking of keeping a good hotel."

The Bustling City

During1866 Omaha was a city bursting with activity. Out on the railroad construction crews became better organized, supplies began to flow to them, and they moved steadily up the Platte Valley.

As railroad construction moved westward along the Platte River, Omaha flourished as the gateway for men and material flowing to the construction zone. New businesses of all kinds announced their presence. By the end of 1867 Omaha boasted 127 saloons, 10 gambling houses, and 25 houses of ill repute.

Twenty-year-old photographer Arundel C. Hull arrived in the center of this frenetic activity. For the next several months, while working as a portrait photographer in the Eaton Gallery, Hull spent his spare time making pictures of various Omaha street scenes and buildings. Field photography at this time was no simple task. It required a heavy tripod and bulky wooden camera, glass plates coated on-the-spot with viscous collodion, a black box to develop and fix the plates, then another process to make each print. Hull became quite adept at field photography around the town. It kept him busy and it was profitable.

Hull's panorama photo of Omaha was taken from Capitol Hill, a favorite spot to record the growth of the city. The present day cityscape shows little resemblance except for the river in the far background.

Omaha's commercial area with its profusion of new businesses grew toward the river front. The three story brick Central Block building housed wholesalers and jobbers for men's wear, dry goods, boots and shoes, paints, oils, glass and crockery, and a bank. The nearby Ware Block, a two-story brick building, also housed wholesalers of liquor, groceries, dry goods, boots and shoes, and a bank. Given this bustling activity, shopkeepers were happy to pose at their front door and most of them bought a print or two from Hull.

Courtesy Union Pacific Railroad Museum.

The Missouri River Bridge when completed in 1872.

The trestles at both ends were soon replaced with massive approach embankments.

The Bridge

From the start of the railroad construction the Missouri River was a major impediment for the Union Pacific. Trainloads of supplies from the east were carried by rail to Saint Louis or Saint Joseph. There they were loaded onto steamers and barges for a slow trip up the shoaled and snag infested river channels to the Omaha landing. Later a railroad connection reached a ferry landing directly across the river from Omaha where materials could more easily be ferried across. But a bridge across the Missouri River was clearly needed. Its location and its financing became the subject of great competition and speculation.

Despite the controversies the flow of construction materials had to continue. As the winter of 1867 approached, the river froze over. Planks were laid out to create a crossing for freight wagons and teams. In December 1867 the need became more urgent and a temporary "ice bridge" was constructed between ferry landings. As soon as the ice was thick enough to support equipment, temporary piles were driven through it. Wooden stringers and beams were then laid across the tops of the piles and rails strung out atop the timber. Lightly loaded trains inched their way across and the crucial flow of supplies continued. In the spring as the thaw began workers raced to reclaim the rails and timber before the ice broke up. Similar bridges were built in 1868 and 1869, and on at least one occasion the river won the race and claimed the bridge in the spring.9,10

Railroad 1869 through Nebraska

When plans for a permanent Missouri River railroad bridge were announced, disputes escalated over its location. After a flurry of competitive inducements Omaha was selected as the bridge location and the Boomer Bridge Company of Chicago was awarded the contract to build it. In less than a year Boomer "busted" and forfeited the contract.[11] The project languished. In 1869 after the Union Pacific and Central Pacific railroads joined rails at Promontory, Utah the value of the bridge for the construction effort passed, but a bridge was still needed for long term operations.

Early in 1870 the American Bridge Company of Chicago took over the project. After a two year construction effort the last truss section was swung into place. The bridge stood as an impressive structure, 2,750 feet long and 60 feet high. Before acceptance, the bridge was tested with a string of ten flat cars, each loaded with 30 tons of stone. Five empty "sacrificial" flat cars followed the loaded cars, and they in turn were followed by a pusher locomotive. The loaded cars were slowly nudged across the bridge. The train stopped eleven times so that the loaded cars sat momentarily at the center of each 250-foot-long truss. The locomotive pushed from a safe position behind the empty cars. One by one as each of the trusses was tested the locomotive let out a long celebratory whistle that was picked up and repeated by other locomotives in the vicinity. When the test train successfully crossed the bridge, a cacophony of whistles celebrated the true completion of the transcontinental railroad.[12]

Photograph by Eugene Arundel Miller.
The Winding Elkhorn River.

3. Elkhorn Station and Fremont

Out on the line laborers were scarce, as was the cash to pay them. The men were unorganized and poorly supervised, but the construction crews finally broke out of the eastern part of Nebraska and turned westward.

The top railroad officials were now focused on raising funds and were less inclined to manipulate the route location for their personal benefit.

Out On the Line

In August 1865 they organized a "corps of engineers" (surveyors) and sent them miles ahead of the construction. Their primary task was to search out and stake the best rail alignment to minimize curves and

29

grades. Next they were to find the most favorable locations for the bridges, and other stream crossings.

The corps comprised a crew of about fifteen men: the surveyors and assistants, teamsters and cooks. They were outfitted with surveying equipment, several wagons, and five tents. They had provisions, but for their extended travel they were pretty much on their own.

One of the members of that corps was an adventuresome 21-year-old Arthur N. Ferguson who signed on as a rod man.13 Ferguson's journals described their travel through the small, pretty valley of Papillion and along the 70-foot-high bluff overlooking the Elkhorn River. "The stream is one of the most crooked and winding I ever saw. By its turns sometimes going a distance of nearly a mile and making a gain of only a few hundred feet." In August 1865 the corps crossed the Elkhorn River on a military bridge "of rough wood work" and then repeatedly got their teams and wagons stuck in the muddy valley bottom. "We managed to get through by doubling teams and shoveling out wheels of the wagons."14

In the fall the construction crews laboriously spread ties and pulled rails around the oxbow, past Bellevue and up West Papillion Creek. There the railroad planned their Elkhorn Station. The officials were somewhat surprised, however, when they found their intended station site and 40 acres of the nearby land preempted by a Mr. William Janney. He and other foresighted private interests had been busy. They had already laid out a town and sold lots. Moreover, they built houses and erected a general store. The town was born. Railroad officials had not realized they lost control of the land value they created but were now alerted to guard against future land grabs.[15,16]

The town's post office, first named "Chicago," engendered predictable confusion. The name was changed to "Elkhorn," even though there was already an Elkhorn City. The post office then changed its name to "Douglas." Finally, the railroad and the town stuck with the name Elkhorn, and ultimately the post office conformed.[17]

Photograph by Arundel C. Hull.
Elkhorn Station, view to the Northeast 1867.
The dirt road at the left is the future Main Street.

Crossing a low divide west of the town railroad crews bridged the Elkhorn River and moved up the valley. By grading up the valley bottom the railroad avoided heavy earthwork, but the progress was agonizingly slow. The tracks reached the existing village of Fremont at the end of December 1865, then winter set in and frozen ground brought construction to a halt.

Railroad 1869 through Nebraska

The community of Fremont was organized and settled as a "company" town ten years before the arrival of the railroad. It was one of several towns set up by private companies to encourage settlement and development of areas thought to hold great promise. The companies often organized transportation for their members and helped them acquire land, build houses, and market their crops. Within a year of the company's arrival at Fremont, the settlers built thirteen log houses.18 To attract more settlers the new town offered free land, free timber for building cabins, and free firewood for a year. Those settlers who stayed the next few years benefited from a stagecoach line connecting them with Omaha, and, at the end of 1865 they excitedly greeted the arrival of the Union Pacific Railroad. In the following years the town thrived as a connecting point for branch railroads.

A Needed Shakeup

When the year 1865 ended barely 40 miles of track were complete but the crews had also finished grading 60 miles farther west. When winter shut down construction, material was on hand for only the next twenty miles. The enabling law required that 100 miles of track be completed by the next June with a fully operating regular passenger and freight service. Considering the disorganization and meager results thus far, the outlook seemed bleak. From New York Doc Durant attempted to keep himself in charge of everything. He faced a huge task of directing surveys and engineering, acquiring supplies, and contracting the actual work. He was unable to delegate, would frequently change his mind, and spent money wastefully at a great rate. In short, Doc Durant was bringing the entire effort to the verge of collapse.

In the early months of 1866, other railroad officials became acutely aware of the need for major changes. Inept Herb Hoxie was relieved of his construction assignment and sent to purchase supplies and arrange for their transport. Samuel Reed, previously in charge of surveys, was elevated to Engineer of Construction and Superintendent of Operations. In a key move the railroad contracted with the Casement Brothers to lay rails. As a former Brigadier General, John Casement fit perfectly as the field leader. Brother Dan ("five feet, nothing" tall) was the organizer and bookkeeper. Both men were hard-bitten, fearless no-nonsense, dawn-to-dusk, drivers.

In one of Doc Durant's best moves he persuaded General Grenville M. Dodge to join the construction effort as Chief Engineer. Dodge insisted on absolute control and, after initially resisting the arrangement, Durant acquiesced and agreed.

The generals set about to organize the work as they would an army campaign. Fortunately, there were a large number of recently discharged soldiers seeking work. They were hired on and organized as they had been in the Army. During the previous year the construction workers were required to bring their housing with them: tents, and boards for shanties. There had to be a better way. The Casements set up an entire train as a rolling construction camp. In the Omaha shops the Casements directed carpenters to build four unique 88-feet-long rail cars. They were outfitted as bunkhouses, with bunks three tiers high, a kitchen, and "dining" space. At the end of the train was the Casements' rolling office with an impressive ceiling rack for hundreds of Army-issue rifles. Standard boxcars were added to the train and outfitted as a bakery, a butcher's car, a pantry for edibles, and other supplies.19 The arrangement revealed the Casements' talent for tight organization. It was designed to keep crew supervision and support close to the front line of construction and helped keep the workers from straying.

Photograph by Arundel C. Hull.
Fremont, 1867.
This is the first known view of Fremont.

A supply base was established in Fremont to stockpile material for the forthcoming season. The "Elk Horn" and other UP river boats and barges were bringing material to Omaha; from there materials began arriving at Fremont: ties, rails, spikes, fishplates, bolts, picks, shovels, and all manner of incidentals. With General Dodge and the Casement Brothers taking charge, the accumulated supplies were quickly moved out to the end of the line. The supply base at Fremont lasted only a matter of weeks. Early in the spring of 1866 as the railhead advanced and the track crews moved westward stockpiles were also moved forward. Later as construction moved on across Nebraska, mountains of supplies grew overnight at Columbus, Fort Kearny, and North Platte, and then disappeared within a few weeks. The construction crews consumed material at a voracious rate.

An Operating Railroad

The Union Pacific was anxious to show the government and investors they had an operating railroad. Freight and passenger service to Fremont was started as soon as the construction crews moved on west. There was a constraint, however, that made itself apparent from the very beginning. The railroad was built as a single track system, as were most of the railroads in the eastern part of the country. But they needed to accommodate two-way traffic. For trains to pass, one of them had to move onto a siding and wait. A telegraph order system and complex traffic rules were developed, but there were always mistakes and mix-ups.

Accidents were frequent both from the conflicts between traffic in opposing directions and also from the lack of construction quality. The hastily laid rails were often crooked and uneven causing cars to lurch from side to side and derail. Occasionally, accidents were reported in an eastern newspaper, but usually they were ignored.

Since the railroad was unfenced, wild game and livestock often wandered across the rails and into the pathway of moving trains. An early accident (of the few actually reported) was near Fremont where a train hit a cow when she refused to move out of the way in time. Several cars flew off the track and overturned. Five men were killed and twelve wounded, and "several ladies were badly mangled."[20] The newspaper reported the incident once but made no further mention of either the injured passengers or the cow.

In the spring of 1867, the young photographer Arundel Hull heaved his wet-plate camera paraphernalia and himself aboard a west-bound train out of Omaha. His first stop was at two-year-old Elkhorn Station. He trudged up the slope from West Papillion Creek, set up his tripod and camera, and took the first known photograph of the village. Without much else of interest to photograph and having sold only one or two prints, he packed up and moved on.

When Hull got off the train at Fremont, only eighteen miles down the line from Elkhorn, he felt encouraged. It was only a village but the town seemed active and welcoming. He set up his camera to take several views, sold a few prints, and again moved on. Hull liked Fremont and after three more years of traveling he chose Fremont for his permanent home.

Photograph by Russell. Courtesy Union Pacific Railroad Museum.
Columbus viewed from the windmill tower.

4. Columbus

To meet the next Congressional deadline the Union Pacific railroad needed to have 100 miles of track completed with regular passenger and freight service operating by July 1, 1866. That milepost was about eight miles west of Columbus.

Once General Dodge had taken over as Chief Engineer and recruited the experienced Casement Brothers as rail contractors, he lost no time in reorganizing his construction forces into an "army" and split the work into manageable parts: bridge builders, graders, and track layers.

UNION PACIFIC RAIL ROAD.

TIME TABLE

For Construction Trains,

TO TAKE EFFECT

MONDAY, JUNE 11TH, 12 O'CLOCK NOON.

STATIONS.	Going West.		Going East.	
	TRAIN No. 1.	TRAIN No. 2.	TRAIN No. 3.	TRAIN No. 4.
OMAHA,	12.00 M.	6.00 P. M.	8.15 P. M.	4.30 A. M.
PAPILLION,	1.30 P. M.	**7.20** "	**7.20** "	3.30 "
ELKHORN,	3.00 "	9.00 "	6.00 "	2.15 "
FREMONT,	**4.30** "	10.30 "	**4.30** "	12.50 "
NORTH BEND,	5.45 "	**11.40** "	3.00 "	**11.40** P. M.
SHELL CREEK,	6.50 "	12.50 A. M.	1.40 "	9.50 "
COLUMBUS,	8.00 "	2.00 "	12.00 M.	8.00 "

THE FULL-FACED FIGURES DENOTE MEETING PLACES.

RULES & REGULATIONS:

1. The Clock in the Cashier's Office at Omaha will be the standard time, and Conductors will regulate their time pieces by it.

2. Trains going West will have the right to Track for one hour behind time. If not then at meeting point, Trains going East will proceed, keeping one hour behind card time until meeting Westward bound Train.

3. At meeting points Conductors will allow five minutes for variation of time if Trains due have not arrived.

4. Trains going East will Side Track at meeting points.

5. Trains will leave Omaha and Columbus on time whether Trains due have arrived or not.

Sam'l B. Reed,

OMAHA, JUNE 9th, 1866.   General Superintendent.

Courtesy Platte County Museum.

Time Table - Omaha to Columbus 1866.

Getting It Together

The newly organized "corps of engineers," the surveyors, were well along setting the route alignment, marking the grade for the road bed, and selecting the best locations for the creek and river crossings. The first surveyors had arrived at Columbus in early August

1865. The party of fifteen was camped for several days at the "pleasant little village situated on the banks of the Loup Forks River." Arthur Ferguson noted in his diary this was "in the midst of a rich farming country which, when fully developed, will be of vast and wonderful wealth." The party spent several days getting ready at Columbus. Fearing that they would find little more usable wood, they went along the river cutting saplings and small trees, shaping them into hundreds of survey stakes. They fully loaded their stake wagon and moved on westward.[21]

Resuming work in 1866, the surveyors searched for hours along the brushy river banks for the stakes left the preceding year. At the Loup River one of the rod men stripped down and swam the icy water to the west side. After crashing through the brush, and with great relief, he finally found the stakes that marked the end of the prior year's work. The rest of the party, wagons, horses, and all, moved up river and crossed on a pontoon bridge built for the U. S. Army. The Army's bridge was a series of wooden boats, lined up side by side across the river and tied to trees on the river bank. Planks placed across the top provided a narrow and somewhat risky roadway. However, the bridge was quite a convenience for the surveyors, the last such convenience they would enjoy for the remainder of the year.[22]

General Dodge's "army" of construction workers followed the surveyors, sometimes several months later. Leading the construction forces were the grading crews: platoons of shovelers. They advanced across the level Platte Valley bottom land clearing the right-of-way of prairie grass and occasional small trees. The terrain was favorable, needing only shallow excavations and small fills to create the roadbed.

In the process the graders used dozens of Ames Brothers shovels and other tools. The Ames Brothers company was a major manufacturer of hand tools in New England. The brothers had accumulated great wealth from the shovel market during the Gold Rush years as well as during the just-ended Civil War. The two Ames were early investors in the Union Pacific Railroad effort and in 1865, when the whole enterprise was in jeopardy for lack of money, they rescued it with major additional financing.

At rivers and streams the surveyors selected bridge locations. Once General Dodge gave approval, bridge builder L. B. Boomer sent its crews out to erect temporary crossings using bridge timbers precut in its Chicago yard. The crossings had to be ready for rails before track laying crews reached them. At most of the crossings the Boomer crews built minimal wooden trestles with beams spanning between the bents and only cross ties to support the rails; no deck, no side rails. Although they were simple, they used a large amount of timber, timber that was scarce and expensive, and had to be dragged long distances to the crossings.

The bridge across the Elkhorn River was the first bridge of significance. The crossing required multiple spans and with untrained crews was difficult to erect. The bridge across the Loup River Forks west of Columbus posed even more of a challenge. Boomer crews tackled it in the early spring with the river full of ice-laden runoff, a challenging construction obstacle. As the grading crews moved well beyond the Loup River Forks the track layers were being organized and energized by the Casement Brothers. There could be no delay with a bridge crossing. In one of the early manifestations of the railroad's mantra "build it fast, fix it later," the Boomer crew struggled to rapidly put up a temporary trestle 1,700 feet long. The track layers crossed it without a change of pace.

The graders and bridge builders were followed by tie crews and track layers. Track layers were the most visibly organized and publicized part of the undertaking. Organization here was the core of the effort and set the pace for all others.

In an effort parallel to the rail layers, separate crews constructed a telegraph line along the edge of the railroad right-of-way. They planted poles and strung wire line at a pace with the track layers. Wherever the Casements' work train stopped overnight, the telegraph crew ran a temporary connection to his rail car construction office so they could keep tabs on the flow of supplies and send telegraph reports of their progress.

Last in the parade of workmen stretching westward were separate crews who erected the Union Pacific station facilities. Many locations along the line were merely marked with a sign. At selected sidings and stations where freight business was anticipated, board station buildings and freight depots were built. At locations where trains needed to take on water, well diggers sunk shafts, then built windmills and water tanks.

As the Casement's crews worked their way from Fremont to Columbus their routine became well organized and they advanced the rails nearly two miles a day. A continuing constraint to their progress was a persistent shortage of ties. Construction forces devoured about 3,000 ties each mile! Crews of contracted wood cutters scoured the Nebraska "forests" for the trees to cut into wood ties and bridge timbers. Timber came from up and down the river, wherever they could be found.

On May 28 1866, Samuel Reed, originally the Chief of Surveys then later Chief of Construction, telegraphed Doc Durant, "Track laid to west end of station at Columbus" and on May 31, Reed telegraphed, "Eight thousand feet of track laid today..."[23] They finally had gotten it together!

A Short Stop for Whiskey
Columbus, Nebraska was founded as a "company" town similar to Fremont. In 1858 a group from Columbus, Ohio anticipated the construction of the transcontinental railroad and correctly speculated that it would run up the wide Platte River valley. A group of thirteen Ohioans organized themselves and headed west. They walked across eastern Nebraska to the confluence of the Platte and Loup Rivers where they

started their settlement with a single log cabin. The settlers soon added other cabins, but more importantly they built a saw mill, a grist mill, and a brewery. The settlement became an Overland Stage station and grew into a thriving little town prior to the arrival of the railroad.

In the spring of 1866 after the railroad construction moved west from Fremont, Columbus was the first settlement the crews reached that had whiskey for sale. It was a "hard place" for the hard working crew, and the men "had a big drunk, with two days lost."[24] There wasn't much time outside of the long workdays, and nothing for the men to spend their money on except liquor.

Photograph by Russell. Courtesy Union Pacific Railroad Museum.

Main Street Columbus, about 1868, in the vicinity of present day 12th Street.

Durant knew that this problem could only get worse. He telegraphed construction boss Reed, "It will not answer to have men so near the whiskey shops in Columbus." From his headquarters in the east, Doc thought they could head off the problem by building a sidetrack west of the Loup Fork and setting up a second materials base there where the men might be contained.

The siding was put in but it did not take long for the whiskey merchants to deliver their merchandise across the Loup River. Once recognized, other opportunists swarmed to the railroad camps and for the next three years the predatory liquor purveyors followed their "captive" customers all the way to Promontory, Utah.

At the end of the two-day drunk in Columbus, the Casement brothers dried out the crews and the track laying operation was quickly brought back up to speed. They succeeded in reaching the 100th mile by June 4, 1866, a month ahead of the Congressional deadline. The Casements proved to be the right men for the job!

Winter

During the winter of 1866-67 while crews were wintering at North Platte, severe winter storms and prolonged freezing hit the entire region. Most rivers, including both the Platte and Loup Rivers, froze solid. Upstream it piled up against railroad embankments and then overtopped them. In some places huge chunks of ice even covered the rails themselves.

Photographer unknown. Nina Hull Miller Collection.
**Ice flowing down the Loup River overtopped the
embankments.**

In the spring the ice on the Loup River broke up and
massive flows moved down the river, slamming into the
bridge. There the ice piled up against the bridge before
splitting into packs and roaring on down the river.

Photographer unknown. Nina Hull Miller Collection.

**In 1867 Ice Breakers were erected
to protect the newly constructed wagon bridge
across the Platte River.**

When Arundel Hull briefly stopped at Columbus in the summer of 1867 the railroad's supply dumps were empty and railroad construction crews were far to the west. Searching Columbus for views that would make good saleable photographs he chose to photograph the new wagon bridge. There were only scattered customers among the wagons, buggies, and horseback riders. After a few sales Hull loaded himself and his gear aboard the next west-bound train.

Nina Hull Miller Collection.

Building the railroad: the teamsters, tie bucks, track layers, gaugers, and spikers.

5. Grand Island

Le Grande Isle was named by an early French fur trader who, in the late 1700s, used the 40 mile long island in the Platte River as a landmark.[25]

In the late 1850s three Iowans, sensing the potential of the Platte Valley area, and the likelihood of a future railroad, formed a town company and recruited settlers.

Le Grande Isle

The Iowans induced thirty Germans to leave Davenport, Iowa and move west to establish a settlement. They picked a location along the old emigrant road on the north side of the river. It was already known as Le Grand Isle.[26] There the settlers determinedly built their cabins and set about to break the sod and plant crops. They hauled their meager harvest to market along the wagon road east to the Missouri River. Although telegraph lines connected the village in 1857, the long and difficult wagon road was a severe constraint to the village's growth. The settlers survived bankruptcy of the town company and waited more than a decade in expectation of a railroad.

In August 1865 as the rail crews struggled to reach Elkhorn, the Union Pacific surveyors passed near Le Grand Isle staking out about ten miles of railroad line each day. Each morning as the survey crews started along the line their teamsters and cooks broke camp and moved it ahead also. Toward the end of each day the survey crew had to search to find their camp. Fortunately, the white canvas of their tents usually made the new camp visible, but on occasion the surveyors were obliged to search for several hours; sometimes it was well after dark before they found it.[27]

In his diary survey crewmember Arthur Ferguson described the huge prairie dog towns they passed along the Wood River. "For miles and miles the ground is completely covered with their huts or holes and on most of them, as far as the eye can reach, you will see them sitting upright on their haunches. Some of our men used to eat them, but I never liked to venture that far."[28]

Great Progress

In the spring of 1866 construction crews moved out of their Fremont winter quarters and worked their way westward through Columbus. The supply line from the east became more effective and the Casement brothers continued to refine their construction organization. They created a series of separate crews, each crew, in sequence, doing a series of very specific jobs. The grading crews, with their Ames Brothers shovels, moved briskly out along the line of stakes left by the surveyors, and shoveled dirt from each side to build up a roadway along the centerline.

Next in line were the tie men. As the construction approached Le Grande Isle the supply of hardwood ties from the east and burnetized ties from Omaha became critically insufficient. As an expedient the railroad sent wood cutters out to harvest cottonwood trees from the heavy stands growing on the Platte River islands. The use of cottonwood was purely a short time solution however, since the soft wood would hold the spikes for only a few years before rotting out. Time and first cost were of overriding importance; "We'll replace them later" was the prevailing promise. (In less than a decade thousands of ties had to be replaced.)

Where they felled trees the wood cutters cut the green logs into ties, eight foot lengths with two flat sides and rough cut ends, and stacked them along the route. Teamsters hauled the ties to the graded roadway and dropped them along the prepared roadbed. Tie bucks then spaced them out, leveled them, and mounded dirt over their centers. As the tie bucks moved forward they were followed by the next platoon of workers. This crew moved along the line with wagons loaded with spikes and steel plates, dropping the exact number of spikes needed at the end of each tie. At 26-foot-long intervals they dropped off splice plates and bolts. Next the work train pushed rail-ladened flat cars as close as possible to the end of the already completed track. Steel rail sections were unloaded from both sides of the railroad cars and onto horse drawn carts and trundled forward along each side of the roadbed. There track crew members pulled a section of rail off each side of the cart, ran the pair of rails ahead and dropped them into place. When a cart was empty they tipped it off to the side and moved the next cart up into place.

Bolters fastened the rail sections together with splice plates. Gaugers aligned the rails, making sure of the spacing, and the spikers drove home a spike, one into each tie alongside each rail... three blows, per spike, 10 spikes per rail.[29] As General "Jack" Casement watched the operation he added men to the crews and replaced the slow ones so that all crews moved relentlessly along at the same speed without a pause. The operation developed rhythm as it was repeated over and over again, and then picked up speed, a thirty-second cycle, 400 rails per mile. Follow-up crews drove in the remaining spikes and shoveled ballast in between the ties. The pay was good: $2.50 to $4 a day depending on the job.

The First Indian Encounter
In early 1866 as the railhead approached Le Grand Isle a group of seventeen Brule Sioux warriors and their leader Spotted Tail rode up from the river to confront the work train. Erasmus Lockwood, Dan Casement's young brother-in-law, described the memorable encounter. "I have always thought they came on a spying expedition. However, our superintendent received them cordially and showed them the process of track laying in all its aspects. They were taken through

the boarding cars at which time they discovered the U.S. rifles stacked horizontally in the roofs. It was interesting to see the expressions on their faces when they discovered these guns. I was following them and noticed one Indian put his hand out the window and measure the thickness of the wall of the car. As he looked at another Indian I could imagine hearing him say, 'I wonder if the bullet could go through?[30]

The Indian visitors were shown through the butcher's car with the hanging sides of beef and the baker's car with ovens and plentiful sacks of flour. After their winter of hunger the Sioux were impressed. Back down the tracks someone suggested that the Sioux show them how accurately they could use their bow and arrows. "I put a shovel upright in the ground about 60 feet away.... Sixteen Indians put their arrows through the hole in the handle, while the seventeenth (Indian) hit the handle at the hole knocking the shovel over. He felt quite disgraced."[31]

"The railroader proposed a new contest: a race between the Indian ponies and the locomotive. The Sioux readily agreed. Spotted Tail was at first reluctant to ride in the engine cab; finally, he agreed and climbed aboard. The Indians lined abreast for the word to go and away they went. At first they outdistanced the locomotive which so pleased them that they gave an Indian war whoop. "Before long the engine gathered speed and easily out ran them. As he passed them the locomotive engineer opened his whistle which so startled them that they swung to the off side of their ponies, hanging on with their left legs over the back. Of course the incident ended the race and the Indians, much crestfallen returned to the boarding train.

"It was only good manners and customary of the Plains Indians that the hosts give food and presents to their guests. The Sioux had to prompt the railroaders, who set out an abundance of food, but in fear of being poisoned, they would not eat anything until the railroaders had tasted it all. They then devoured everything in sight.

"Things turned ugly. The Indian demanded that their ponies be loaded with sacks of flour and quarters of beef. The superintendent refused his demand saying that they could have all they wanted to eat but could not carry any away. Spotted Tail threatened to come over some night with three thousand warriors and clean us out. The superintendent told the interpreter to tell Spotted Tail what he was going to say. He put his doubled fist against Spotted Tail's nose and let out a string of oaths such as I never heard before. Spotted Tail made no answers, but all mounted their ponies and rode away. That was the last we ever saw of them. They had seen our guns! However, fearing they might return, we doubled our night patrol for some weeks."[32]

Photograph by Arundel C. Hull.

Grand Island 1867.
The view is to the south across Front Street. The small building left of the saloon is the Post Office. The O.K. store is in the right foreground, the Roman Catholic Church is in back.

A Town is Born

In the spring of 1866, as the first railroad survey crews moved on far to the west other survey crews arrived and laid out street and lots for the new town of Grand Island. The new town was about a mile north of the original settlement. After their experience at Elkhorn, railroad officials were disinclined to give anyone else the opportunity to file on unclaimed land and subdivide it to profit from the railroad's presence. The Union Pacific Railroad even launched an early promotional effort to stimulate the sale of their lots by having several houses prefabricated in Chicago, then shipped out and erected in the new town.

By mid-year the rails reached Grand Island. The first depot was a tent which was also the railroad land agent's office. Nearby was a small boarding house for railroad employees. The town of Grand Island became "official" in November of 1866 when a Postmaster was appointed and a post office building erected.

Flood, then Fire

The winter of 1866-67 brought an unusually large snowfall and low temperatures throughout the plains and the mountains to the west. In a telegram to the officials back east Construction Chief Reed advised, "I expect very high water, and we may lose some bridges." They were warned but, of course, there was little they could do but to brace themselves. Then came spring rains with the snow melt and ice break up. The river rose to the highest level ever seen. Near Grand Island the Platte River left its channel and surged over its banks in a mad arc leaving two wide gaps in the rails and embankments.[33] In some places the embankments were entirely gone, leaving the track and ties dangling. Elsewhere the tracks were gone and the embankments left behind.

In a later telegram to Doc Durant, Reed reported flooding of the whole length of the railroad and immense damage to road. Miles of railroad were damaged and the Prairie Creek bridge carried away but surprisingly all the other bridges withstood the surging flood and ice."[34]

In April 1867 as the railroad crews struggled to repair the flood damage, young Arthur Ferguson reported to work in Omaha. There he intended to board a train for North Platte where he would rejoin his survey crew. However, he was stuck! He wrote in his diary, "Water in the rivers still rising... risen four inches since last night." He waited. A week later he boarded a train and got as far as Elkhorn where the railroad bridge had been damaged and was not yet passable. He was ferried across the swollen channel to the tracks on the opposite side. There he caught a train loaded with supplies, largely baled hay destined for the construction teamsters' horses. The train inched its way across new embankments and repaired track. It rolled on westward through the night but early in the morning one of car-loads of hay caught fire: a spark from the locomotive having set it off. Ferguson noted in his diary, "It was a great sight to see an engine rushing madly across the plains, followed by a car wrapped in flames and streaming sparks and fire in its path." The two other cars caught fire, "and we had to run with those burning cars some ten or twelve miles."[35]

The flood and fire excitement was well past when photographer Arundel Hull arrived in Grand Island that fall. He climbed off the train to explore the town. After a brief walk about, he found the best spot for his photograph here was from atop a railroad car parked on a side track. He made repeated trips up the ladder on the side of the car to haul up his camera and sensitized glass plates. With his perseverance he captured what is believed to be the earliest known photograph of the new town. Hull sold several prints of the panorama and views of Locust Street but soon "sold out the market." After a day or two with no more customers he again boarded a west-bound train for the next step of his adventure. Hull photographed the O. K. Store, owned by Koenig and Wiebe. The store was built, in 1862, at the original Le Grande Isle settlement. There the building was fortified for protection of the settlers during the Sioux and Cheyenne War. The building had corner rifle towers and was walled in with breastworks of sod. In 1867, shortly before Hull's photograph, the owners moved the building into the town, at Front and Locust streets.

The Roman Catholic Church was built soon after the town was laid out but only four years later it was blown down in a storm. The stalwart parishioners rebuilt it at the same location, the corner of Second Street and Walnut.

Photograph by Carbutt. Courtesy Union Pacific Railroad Museum.

Grand Island roundhouse and freight depot, 1870.
Note the workmen posing on the turntable.

When the railroad designated Grand Island as their first division point it triggered a flurry of construction activity. The railroad's main building was an impressive roundhouse ready to house and maintain several new locomotives. Various other railroad shops and an "eating house" were soon in place. Grand Island had a vigorous beginning and the railroad presence continued to fuel its growth. By 1870 Grand Island became a robust railroad town.

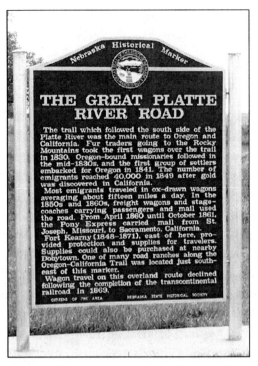

A marker on the route of early westward bound travelers.

6. Kearney Station

In the spring of 1866 construction crews pushed westward out of Columbus and the survey crews were sent out miles ahead of them across the prairie.

In July 1866 Ferguson joined a new survey party to stake out work for the construction crews. The work was in the "Third 100 miles" between the western end of La Grand Isle out to the confluence of the South and North Platte Rivers.

57

Out Across the Prairie

The surveyor's camp was initially set up near present day Elm Creek. From there Ferguson and his fellow surveyors traveled up and down the line staking locations for the bridge builders and graders and measuring the contractor's completed work.

In his diary Ferguson usually made a daily record of the weather: often unpleasant and frequently surprising. He wrote the days were "extremely warm... We have had no rain to speak of for a month and almost everything is dry and parched." Four days later they were nearly burned out by a prairie fire, undoubtedly started by a lightning strike. "While on our way up this afternoon, we could see vast volumes of heavy smoke rolling upwards, while underneath the lurid glow, and darkening aspect of the coming storm. It presented a sublime scene. The earth in every direction now presents a black charred and desolate appearance. It is a gloomy night and I am sitting in my wet tent with no shirt on under my coat... outside it looks dark, and the heavy rain is pouring down in torrents on our canvas."[36]

All through the summer the weather kept them nimble. At the end of July he wrote, "Last night we had a severe rain storm which came very near giving us a good wetting. I chanced to wake just in time to alarm the camp and make preparation for it as our tent was in the condition it had been during the day with the walls fastened up to give free ventilation." Then early in August, "This afternoon we were visited by another severe storm, with vivid lightning and heavy thunder and wind. One of the tents was completely blown to the ground by the violence of the wind. A storm on the plains is sublime... reminding one of the power and might of Him..."[37]

The weather was not the only thing that kept the surveyors on edge. "Felt very nervous about Indians, as we are in the vicinity of where the worst troubles occurred during the late Indian War; and we are almost entirely without arms or ammunition." Although the camp was only a few miles from the garrison at Fort Kearny they were on the opposite side of the river and unlikely to find that soldiers would afford any real protection.

For young Arthur Ferguson many aspects of the life out along the railroad were quite different from the life back in town. Ferguson wrote of being kept awake at night by the owls as they went on frequent night time hunts. Then he reported grasshoppers, "Today the air seemed perfectly alive with grasshoppers. They were so numerous, that they could be compared with a snow storm of insects." As the surveyors moved across Nebraska, Ferguson frequently wrote of the herds of antelope. Usually the surveyors watched the herds in the distance but occasionally the animals came near, "We saw a large herd of antelope in the morning that did not seem to pay any very great regard to our presence."[38] On occasion some of the surveyors' party would hunt the antelope for fresh meat, but the animals seemed to sense their intent. Only now and then were the hunters successful.

As the surveyors and grading crews worked their way westward the track layers were always pressing them from behind. During August the railroad track layers spiked down their steel, marking "stations" as they went: Alda, Wood River, Shelton, Gibbon Switch, and Buda, and the newly designated Fort Kearney Station.[39] A rail siding and switch was built at Gibbon as a supply terminus for Fort Kearny. A house was built nearby for the section hands. However, the Fort was seven miles south and eight miles west of Gibbon and it was across the bifurcated river and Le Grand Isle. Gibbon was a lonesome outpost, nothing but prairie grass. The trees had all been cut for ties and the nearest hill was eight miles away. The railroad built the Gibbon Switch to serve the Fort but the Fort Commander, General Gibbon, elected to use the next station down the line, Fort Kearny Station (later renamed Buda) to receive supplies. Here the railroad was only five miles from the Fort and the river was more easily forded.

Five years after the Fort and the Gibbon Switch were bypassed, an organized company of ex-soldiers, "Soldiers Free Homestead Colony of Ohio," arrived to establish their colony, the origin of today's town of Gibbon.[40]

What about Fort Kearny and Dobytown?

Fort Kearny was one of the earliest outposts along the Oregon Trail, the second Army post named for General Stephen Watts Kearny.[41] It was located on a slight rise about a mile from the south bank of the river out of the reach of frequent flooding. Several immigrant trails from the Missouri River converged into the "Great Platte River Road" at this location. There was a heavy stand of timber nearby and grass for animals. For thousands of Forty-Niners and other emigrants the Fort provided a welcome respite after their first 200 miles on the trail.

Here emigrants could re-supply, find a blacksmith for wagon repairs, and prepare for the trail ahead. More important, if Indian troubles were expected the emigrants could be held at the Fort to form up protective wagon trains before venturing further.

As the Fort grew it boasted both a post office and a newspaper. The qualifications for Postmaster were only slightly more than a demonstration of literacy and, when the application for the post office was sent in, "Kearny" was mistakenly spelled with an "e." The application came back approved and that spelling has persisted, except for the name of the Fort itself.

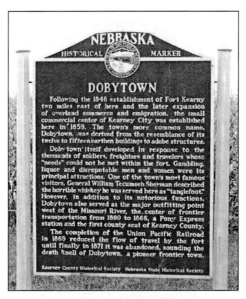

**The site of Dobytown,
six miles southeast of present Kearney.**

Two miles west of the Fort a small trading center, Dobytown, sprang up with a handful of sod and adobe "houses." An Omaha newspaper described it as a collection of "huts and hovels" with more saloons than families.

Of the sod houses..."Me walls are thick...but not impervious to snakes...which frequently bivouac on the beds....a desolate spot with musquetoes by the bushel and plagued with storms. One could not stand up for fear of being struck by lightning or lie down for fear of being drowned."[42] Lightning could produce eerie effects illuminating everything that stood upright. It stunned and killed both animals and men but its biggest threat was causing a stampede. The choking road dust became axel deep mires after rainstorms, often requiring twelve teams of oxen to pull the wagons out. Yet the Fort was an oasis and "a breather of civilization on the endless prairie."

In one respect it was different from Fort Kearny. Dobytown provided plenty of opportunity to slake travelers' thirst and other pent up desires. It offered the full gambit of temptations: gambling, disreputable women, and horrible whiskey. The "tanglefoot" served at Dobytown was not soon forgotten.

When the Union Pacific laid its tracks along the north side of the river, the posts at Fort Kearny and Dobytown were left stranded on the south side. The Army closed the Fort two years after completion of the railroad. Dobytown likewise shrank and disappeared soon after.[43]

The Real Kearney

In his diary Arthur Ferguson told of the track laying crews moving west close on the heels of the surveyors. His August 21 diary entry noted, "The railroad track is reported as being a mile and a half west of Kearney Station."[44] Within only a few weeks the section house was built five miles west of Kearney Station. It was a primitive cabin made of upright boards but it contained three rooms for the man in charge and a loft for the other hired track workers. For weather protection the entire cabin was enclosed by blocks of sod. The cabin was built on a government section intended to be at the center of the town site and the junction with future railroads to the north and south. The cabin became known as the Junction House, "... a shack 15 feet by 15 feet." A lean-to was added and it later metamorphosed into a two story frame building, the Junction House Hotel.[45]

At Kearney Junction, the railroad set up another temporary materials base. Here they rapidly accumulated all manner of supplies as loaded trains came in from the east and unloaded material into great heaps alongside the tracks. In August 1866 General Dodge reported that they had stockpiled enough iron and ties to build another 100 miles.[46] The railroaders were pushing to reach the confluence of the North and South Platte Rivers before winter.

At Kearney Junction General Dodge had the surveyors lay out the government section in a regular grid of nicely aligned streets and small lots. There was a flurry of interest in the new town and the railroad now set about to raise money by land sales. (It was also seen as an opportunity to skim off some of the "profit.") To

63

attract settlers they made prices quite attractive. A hundred fifty dollars could purchase a nice corner lot. A hundred was all for an inside location. Toward the edge of town prices were even more attractive: $75 and $50. Installment "plans" were OK, one-third down and the balance in two years. There was a caveat: the buyers were to plant shade trees within ten months.

Three years after completion of the Union Pacific's dash across the west, the Burlington and Missouri Railroad built their line up from the south to meet the Union Pacific tracks. In a bit of clever maneuvering the B & M laid out a town on the section east of Kearney Junction.

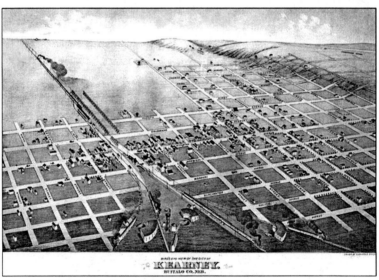

Nina Hull Miller Collection.
Artist's Map of Kearney, circa. 1899.

The Burlington and Missouri Railroad hoped to force the actual railroad junction onto their holdings. The B & M acquired their land with a clever strategy that later became often used by others.

On the target section of land, four insiders filed claims on each of the four quarter-sections. Together the claimants built a four room cabin at the exact center of the section, each room in a different quarter. Ostensibly they lived there for the required time. Once the men had thus "proved up" on the claim, by prearrangement they sold their property to the land company or some other intermediary.

When the Burlington and Missouri Railroad met Union Pacific tracks the UP refused to stop their trains at the B & M junction. Instead the Union Pacific trains continued on to stop at the "Junction House" a mile west. Passengers were much inconvenienced. Later, after many passenger complaints and much hard bargaining, the two railroads arranged a land swap and agreed to use the same station.

Kearney Junction became the first major shipping point for cattle driven up from Texas. That use soon faded as the hardworking settlers grew to dislike the cowboys, who strutted, caroused, and generally tore up the town. As the town's people prepared to run them out, the trail head shifted farther west, giving the problem to more western stations.

At Elm Creek

The prolific prairie dogs spread their colonies in the easily burrowed soil along the Platte Valley. At Elm Creek the surveyors, unwittingly, set up their first camp site in the middle of an immense prairie dog empire. After a few days of aggravation from the rodents' chatter and night time hunts by owls, the surveyors moved their camp a few miles farther west.

Regardless of the prairie dog population the railroad built a station at Elm Creek. (However, the present village is a mile east.) It was the official meal stop for the two daily passenger trains, one in each direction. As the trains eased to a stop at the station the passengers rushed to the eating house run by Charles Davis and his wife Kate. There was a flurry of activity with no time to spare and any complaining passenger was at risk of losing his chance to eat at all. Davis also ran the local saloon, a convenient detour for those who drank their meals.[47]

Station stops were few and far between for train passengers during the early days. Those travelers who relied on strong drink embraced every opportunity offered to lay in a supply of bottles and jugs. The presence of liquor on an emigrant train was especially troublesome for the trainmen. At Elm Creek the station keepers and trainmen had a plan to lessen the evil. On the arrival of an emigrant train the eating-house keepers refused to sell liquor in bottles and jugs, telling the passengers that the trainmen objected but that if they waited they could have all the bottles and jugs of liquor they wished At the last moment those who waited loaded up with wet goods. After the train had left for the west it was discovered that the wet goods consisted of cold tea and for a quarter mile or so west of the station the roadside was littered with broken jugs and bottles."[48]

Leslie's Illustrated Newspaper. Nina Hull Miller Collection.

**A decade after the railroad was completed
prairie dog towns still persisted.**

An Appetite for Timber

Before the railroad came up the Platte Valley large stands of timber extended all along the riverbanks and on the islands between the many river channels. The trees were mainly cottonwood. Although cottonwood was unsuitable for ties and was poor wood for board lumber, timber of any species and size was taken to fuel the railroad locomotives' voracious appetite. Coincidentally, the winter following the railroad construction was especially severe and the absence of the forests, as windbreaks, became of concern. Already the effects of the "clear cut" timber harvesting were being felt.

Railroad 1869 through Nebraska

Even the railroaders saw the problem they had created so, as lots were sold, the buyers were required to plant shade trees within twelve months. The settlers and their new Nebraska neighbors took tree planting to heart and in the next decade or so over ten million trees were planted. Nebraskans continue to celebrate a special day each year, Arbor Day, for tree planting.

> ### The National Arbor Day.
> The lack of trees, in severe contrast to the forested eastern part of the country, led the new settlers to place great importance on the planting of trees to serve as windbreaks, to keep the soil in place, and to give shade from the hot summer sun. J. Sterling Morton, who moved to Nebraska's treeless plains in 1854, was a journalist, editor, and Secretary of the Nebraska Territory. Moreover he was a naturalist and sorely missed the trees he knew at his former home in Detroit. He widely promoted tree planting by individuals, civic organizations and other groups. His proposal for a tree planting holiday called "Arbor Day" was adopted by the State Board of Agriculture, and during the first official Arbor Day, April 10, 1872, over a million trees were planted.
>
> The day became an official Nebraska State holiday.
>
> Source: Arbor Day Foundation

The Frontier Index

Before the railroad crossed Nebraska, Fort Kearny was a lively outpost on the Oregon Trail south of the river. While there seemed to be a great potential at the Fort for a newspaper, that proved not to be the case. After a long struggle newspaper owner, Moses Sydenham gave up and sold the *Fort Kearny Herald* to an unsuspecting and optimistic pair, Hiram Brundage and Seth Mobley, the telegraph operator. The two found that news was sparse and advertising income was near nothing. When a new telegrapher, Leigh Freeman, and his brother Fred arrived and expressed an interest, the owners were happy to unload it. The *Herald* became the Freemans' in December 1865.

As new owners of the *Fort Kearny Herald*, Leigh and Fred proved to be unique to say the least. Leigh Freeman was described as an unreconstructed secessionist. "Bombastic, somewhat eccentric; he was always flamboyant, aggressive and rigidly positive in his belief."[49] The Freeman brothers, sensing the business limitations at the Fort, moved their press first to Dobytown and then to Kearney Junction on the north side of the river. The brothers foresaw a fast dollar for themselves by following the railroad, selling the news to the construction crews and the hundreds of hangers-on, and selling advertising to all those businesses aiming to profit from the same crowd. The paper became *The Frontier Index*, and known as the "newspaper-on-wheels."

In the fall of 1866 Leigh and Fred loaded their press and other paraphernalia on wagons and headed west from Kearney. They apparently stopped briefly at Plum Creek but opted to move on to North Platte. The latter had been designated as the winter terminus of the Union Pacific. It became momentary home to almost four thousand adventurers, all preparing to wait out the winter there. During the Freemans' move to North Platte their wagon train was held up but, according to Fred Freeman, "when the raiders found that the freight was only a printing press, they left in disgust." (The would-be robbers were likely to have been Jack Morrow's men who at that time accosted many travelers approaching within a few miles of North Platte.)

After wintering at North Platte, the Freemans moved west with their *Frontier Index*. They published a few issues in Julesburg, moved to Fort Sanders and then wintered again, this time in Laramie. The Freemans' reported everything of interest without constraint, commenting on those events and people with "extreme candor." They baited other newspapers, zealously criticized politicians they did not like, fearlessly attacked what they perceived as lawlessness, crime, and criminals. In the process they frequently offended some pretty rough characters.

In the following years the Freeman brothers and their *Frontier Index* paused in Benton. They then moved on to Green River and Bear River City, Wyoming Territory. At "Bear City" the newspaper reached its demise, when it was sacked and burned by an outraged mob.

**Granite Marker tells of one savage Cheyenne Indian
attack on a wagon train in the fall of 1864.**

7. Plum Creek (Lexington)

*The graders and bridge builders were miles
ahead of the track layers. They were poorly
armed and rightly concerned about the Indian
threat.*

In early September 1866 Arthur Ferguson's survey
crew was sent on west to the Union Pacific's forth 100
mile section of line. They were to set stakes for grading
crews and bridge builders all the way to the confluence
of the North and South Platte Rivers.

Railroad 1869 through Nebraska

The Indian Threat

After the surveyors broke camp at Elm Creek, they stopped at contractors' camps along the way for meals and to graze their teams, and for reports of Indian activity. As they traveled farther from Elm Creek, and the protection of Fort Kearny, their anxiety increased. Arthur Ferguson wrote about the first night enroute, "Last night we had a dismal time, as it was very cold and damp and we lay on the ground shivering with cold and in fear of Indians. We were but a handful of men, poorly armed, in a strange, wild desolate country with a small and sickly campfire half hidden...to prevent it from being seen by eyes other than our own, who might at that moment be seeking our scalp, the bloody trophy which is so much coveted by the prowling savage."[50]

The surveyors passed along the north side of the Platte River well aware of an Indian attack two years earlier. A wagon train of 10 four-mule teams had stopped south of the river at Daniel Freeman's small trading post and Pony Express station on Plum Creek. A few miles west of the post, 100 Cheyenne and Sioux Indians attacked the wagon train completely encircling it and ransacking it. They massacred all eleven men, then captured and carried off a woman and a nine-year-old boy.[51] Later the same day there were several other Indian attacks on settlers and travelers, including a raid on a nearby ranch. They burned it and drove off the livestock. The "Plum Creek Massacre" gave reason for the survey crews to be particularly nervous.

Rifles Blazing

Following the surveyor's stakes the graders and bridge builders quickly finished their section's work. The track layers followed, moving relentlessly along, stringing out their endless ribbon of rails. When the end of track was only ten miles west of the newly named Plum Creek Station, an Indian war party attacked a work train, took the crew hostage, and torched the wooden cars. The alert telegrapher flashed a message to Grenville Dodge, the Chief Engineer who was with the construction forces out at the end of the line. Dodge was prepared for this kind of thing. He had identified former soldiers among the work force and set up an armory in a car on the work train. The former General quickly rounded up twenty "soldiers" from the work crews and broke out rifles and ammunition. A work engine pulled a couple of boxcars back along the line into the midst of the Indians, where the "soldiers" burst out of the cars with rifles blazing. The startled Indians abandoned their rampaging and all remaining thoughts of looting, and quickly escaped.

The New Plum Creek

In early 1866, anticipating the railroad's arrival, Daniel Freeman was determined to take advantage of the new trade opportunities it would bring. Before the tracks arrived he homesteaded land north of the river close to where he expected the depot building to be located. There he built a two-story log building where he set up a store on the ground floor and living quarters for his family above.

Later in the year as the railroaders passed westward along the north side of the Platte River they named the new station Plum Creek, even though the creek was on the opposite side of the river. After the graders, tie bucks, and track layers passed out of sight to the west, other construction crews moved in to build a depot building, a section house, and coal house. But the Freeman's had their advantage and Mrs. Freeman boarded men in our big new house across from the depot."

Later when Freeman surveyed his land, both he and the railroad were surprised. The depot occupied part of his homestead claim. A land swap seemed to be the answer but negotiations proved fruitless. Freeman and the railroad agents were both stubborn and unable to reach an amicable agreement. However, the railroad had the upper hand. They simply moved the depot a mile west onto their own land. The center of town also moved and this time Freeman was left behind.

Lasso the Beast

The Indians continued to chafe at the presence of the white man and the relentless westward intrusion of the "Iron Horse." Chief Turkey Leg, who led a large tribe of Cheyenne, attempted to stop the railroad's incursion across their lands. He organized fifty of his warriors who prepared a huge rawhide rope. They strung the rope across the tracks and looped the ends around their ponies, then patiently waited. As a freight train steamed down the line the warriors snared it and raced along the track to bring it to a halt. The ponies were no match for the engine and both the animals and warriors were drawn under the iron wheels. The men and ponies were cut to pieces. The failure infuriated the Indians and heightened Turkey Leg's resolve for revenge.

Artist: Theodore N. Kaufmann.
Courtesy Saint Louis Mercantile Library, University of Missouri.

Cheyenne Indians preparing to derail and attack the oncoming train.

Derailed and Killed

In August, a year after the construction crews passed through Plum Creek, a more widely-known Indian attack (often incorrectly referred to as the "Plum Creek Massacre") occurred three and a half miles west of the town.52

Cheyenne scouts, lead by Spotted Wolf, watched from far off ridges observing the construction train's smoke and steam, the swarms of white men, and the ribbons of iron stretching across their land. They returned to their encampment and reported to Chief Turkey Leg that there might be something valuable in the big wagons on the metal road, perhaps clothing or even food. If they could break the wagons open they could take whatever would be useful to the tribe.

Railroad 1869 through Nebraska

Moved to action, Spotted Wolf's party, including a warrior named Porcupine and a friend named Red Wolf, set about to capture one of the "big wagons," and break open the "boxes." Reaching the rail line, they came across a jumble of discarded ties. There they pried up the rails, loosened a joint, and lifted one end of each rail, dragged up several old ties, and pushed them underneath. Pairs of Indian warriors boosted each other up the telegraph poles and yanked the wires down from the insulators. They used the wire, along with some of their own rawhide, to lash the ties and rails all together in a solid bundle. They built a bonfire in the nearby ravine, concealed themselves in the tall grass nearby, and sat down to wait.53

The station keepers at Plum Creek soon discovered the telegraph had gone dead between there and Willow Island. The line required immediate repair since it was the direct link along the entire railroad. Even though it was after dark, William Thompson rolled out a handcar. He and four other workers loaded up wire, tools, and their carbines, and set out to find and repair the break. The handcar crew carried a pair of hurricane lamps and as they pumped the car down the line they watched the reflection of the light on the overhead wires to spot the break. They had not yet found the break in the wire when they saw the bonfire and, rightly fearing an Indian attack, they pumped frantically to get past it. In the dark they failed to see the upturned rails and ties. The handcar crashed into the barricade and flew into the air spilling the five men. The workmen fled down the tracks but the Indians leaped out of the high grass and in quick pursuit caught up with, and killed four of them.

Although Thompson was shot in the arm he continued to flee. One of the Indians pursued him on horseback, overtook him and clubbed him to the ground. "He then took out his knife, stabbed me in the neck and making a twirl around his fingers with my hair, he commenced sawing and hacking away at my scalp. Though the pain was awful, and I felt dizzy and sick, I knew enough to keep quiet. The process seemed to take a half-hour. He gave the last finishing cut to the scalp on my left temple and as it hung a little, gave it a jerk. I just thought then that I could have screamed my life out..." Although the pain was excruciating, Thompson pretended to be unconscious. "I can't describe it to you. It just felt as if the whole head was taken right off." The Indian then remounted his horse and galloped away. He inadvertently dropped the scalp within a few feet of Thompson who, despite his trauma, managed to retrieve it and remain hidden.

Thompson feigned death while the warriors moved about in the dark to plunder the rifles and tools spilled from the handcar. The Indians grabbed the rifles, new breechloaders. The unfamiliar weapons appeared to break in two and seemed useless to the Indians so they threw them away. Meanwhile lying motionless, Thompson listened to the Indians moving around whispering to each other as they piled more ties on the track and wired them together using repair wire from the wrecked handcar.

Porcupine and Spotted Wolf noticed two lights on the eastern horizon and sent two warrior scouts toward the lights to frighten them off. Soon the scouts realized what they were and as they galloped back the first locomotive overtook them. The Indians first shot at the train to stop it, then tried to throw a rope over it, but their ponies were spooked and bolted. At the sound of the Indian gunfire "Bully" Brooks Bower, the engineer of the lead locomotive, the Osceola, ordered more steam and sped up to rush past the attackers.

Thompson had been lying motionless for an hour and a half when he heard the low rumbling sound. He recognized it as an approaching train but he dared not try to flag it since he was still in the midst of the circling Indians. If they saw him move they would most certainly finish him off.

In the dim headlight of the lead engine Bower saw the pried up rails. He immediately "whistled down" for the brakes and reversed the engine, but the train was on a slight downgrade and at thirty-five miles an hour he was unable to stop it. The engine crashed into the barrier and leaped in the air with the following cars crashing one by one into a tremendous heap. "Bully" was ripped open as he was thrown across the throttle lever and through the window of the engine cab. The fireman, "Drummer" Hendershot, who was shoveling in fuel, was thrown bodily into the firebox. The conductor, the brakeman, and two other men who were in the caboose leaped out. When the conductor ran forward to the pileup he saw "Bully" Bower sitting on the ground disemboweled, and "Drummer" being roasted alive. As he raced back to flag the second train, the Indians shot and killed "Bully," the brakeman, and the other two men from the caboose.

The conductor flagged the second train just in time to avoid becoming part of the wreckage. In the dark the train backed down the line three and a half miles to

Plum Creek (Lexington)

Plum Creek where the trainmen tried in vain to rouse the townspeople to help. Fear of the Indians was widespread and no one was willing to risk going after them in the dark.

In the dawn's light a few of the Indians discovered bolts of bright-colored cloth. After tying one end to their ponies' tails they gleefully raced across the prairie with great cloth streamers flying out behind. For the rest of their "take" the attackers looted boxes of footwear, bales of tobacco, cotton and velvet fabric, leather saddles and harness, sacks of flour and coffee, tea, sugar, and the ever present whiskey. For them it was a treasure trove and they raced off with their take long before the rescuers arrived at the scene. After daylight the conductor again tried to round up help at Plum Creek. By mid-morning a small group of men were roused, got themselves armed, and bolstered their courage. When they arrived at the wreck the debris was still burning but the Indians were gone.

During the night while the Indians were preoccupied with looting, William Thompson painfully crawled through the grass still clutching his scalp. In his agony he fled fifteen miles west to the nearest inhabited station at Willow Island. There the station keepers crudely dressed his wounds and brought him to Plum Creek, but there was no legitimate doctor to help anywhere out along the rail line. The nearest doctor was in Omaha so the men laid Thompson out on a mattress in a boxcar and covered him with a sheet. Next to him was his scalp in a bucket of water. The boxcar was coupled to the next east-bound train and arrived in Omaha ten hours later. In Omaha the railroad crew helped him find a doctor. He brought the scalp along and pleaded with the doctor to "reset" it on his head. The doctor apparently tried but the effort failed.[54]

A short time later Thompson talked at length to Henry Morton Stanley who was a reporter for a Saint Louis newspaper. (This was the same Stanley who, a few years later, successfully searched Africa for Dr. Livingston.) "The scalp," reported the observant Stanley, "was about nine inches in length and four in width, somewhat resembling a drowned rat as it floated curled up, on the water." Thompson had his scalp tanned and kept it as he continued to work for the Union Pacific Railroad. He took the scalp with him when he returned to his native England, several years later, and later still he shipped the shriveled piece of tanned scalp back to the Omaha doctor as a gift.

Nina Hull Miller Collection.

The track crews built a side track around the wrecked train and await other crews to recover the locomotive and cars.

Photographer unknown.
Courtesy Union Pacific Railroad Museum.

"Osceola" the locomotive derailed and wrecked at Plum Creek, was rebuilt in Council Bluffs and was back in service a few months later.

The Pawnee Scouts

Earlier, in response to the growing Indian threat, Major Frank North had been authorized to organize a battalion of Pawnee Indian scouts. The Pawnee were traditional enemies of the Sioux and Cheyenne, having been attacked by them many times before. At the time of the Plum Creek derailment small detachments of the Pawnee Scouts were scattered at various stations along the line west of Sidney. When Major North was notified of the attack, he rode to the nearest detachment and within an hour had his men mounted up and headed eastward. When they arrived at the end of the rail line, the men, horses, and wagons were loaded onto a train and steamed east. At Julesburg they attached their cars to a passenger train and by midnight they were at the Plum Creek scene.[55]

The scouts soon joined other Federal troops with orders to disperse any Indians in the area.

Photograph by Arundel C. Hull.
Soldier's tents in front of the freight house at Plum Creek.

The Troops and Scouts chased the Cheyenne for several days but without much success. The Scouts returned to the railroad and camped at Plum Creek and from there made several more unsuccessful forays. After a few weeks they were transferred to North Platte and then to the new town of Cheyenne to better protect the construction crews to the west. 56

The following fall when photographer Arundel Hull arrived at Plum Creek a small Army detachment was still camped there. He felt some degree of protection by their presence and waited several days before venturing farther west. After a brief stop to photograph nearby Willow Island, Hull moved on to the more populated town of North Platte.

Photograph by Carbutt. Courtesy Union Pacific Railroad Museum.
Doc Durant at the end of track, 1866.

8. The Great Excursion and 100th Meridian (Cozad)

In the summer of 1866, the surveyors took full advantage of the terrain to lay out miles of straight lines and flat grades. Despite the summer "scorcher" the Casement Brothers' gangs, prodded by bonuses and other inducements, sweltered on and quickened their ever increasing pace.

The construction crews were able to string out nearly 200 miles of railroad iron in two months and in their wake a string of new sidings and towns were created: Stevenson, Elm Creek, Overton, Josselyn, Plum Creek, and Coyote.

To Celebrate the "Milestone"

In the fall the track crew was approaching the 100th Meridian, a great symbolic marker 245 miles from Omaha. In anticipation of the "milestone" Doc Durant hosted an extravagant promotional trip to carry important invitees out along the line. Of the more than 300 invitations sent to the nation's notables a hundred forty responded.[57] The impressive guest list included three Senators, twelve Congressmen, Todd Lincoln, the Francis Trains, the Silas Seymours, George Pullman, John Duff, and many others.

About 100 of the guests started their trip from New York Monday October 15th. They traveled by rail to Pittsburgh then on to Chicago. At that point the Great Western Light Guard (Oompah) Band boarded their train and accompanied them, musically and otherwise. The group arrived at Saint Joseph, Missouri, Friday evening where they were met by Herb Hoxie, (who had been relieved of his construction contract). Hoxie welcomed the visitors aboard two waiting Missouri River Packet steamers, the Colorado and the Denver. The more refined Rosenblatt's Band of St. Joseph also joined the group and the partiers departed for the two day trip up the Missouri River. Flags were fluttering and both bands playing, along many miles of winding, snag filled, muddy, shoaled waterways. The guests arrived at Omaha Monday morning Oct 22, a week after having left New York City.

Col. Seymour and Omaha officials gathered dockside for a welcome celebration. After the obligatory speeches, carriages carried the guests to the refurbished Herndon House and other hotels about town, or to residences of several local families who were eager to host such important guests. The guests were "astonished to find themselves among people of wealth, refinement, and enterprise."[58] A gourmet banquet and a surprise reception ball were held that evening at the Herndon House with "entertainment" that would do credit to any similar gathering back east.

The following morning most of the men toured the extensive facilities that Union Pacific had constructed at Omaha: a roundhouse for twenty locomotives, a blacksmith shop with twelve forges, a two-story machine shop, car shops that turned out nine cars per week, and more.

Photograph by Carbutt. Courtesy Union Pacific Railroad Museum.
The Excursion train headed west.

On Their Way

The Excursionists' departure for the 100th Meridian was planned for 10 a.m. Two trains were assembled, their locomotives replete with decorative antlers and bunting. On the lead train employees and caterers loaded all the supplies needed for the trip: tents, bedding, buffalo robes, wood for the evening's bonfires, provisions for all the meals, and case after case of champagne. The second train was made up with four brand new passenger coaches and the splendid Director's car (formerly President Lincoln's Funeral Car).[59] The passengers included the dignitaries, their wives, a few servants, three government commissioners, reporters, the two musical groups and the official photographer, John C. Carbutt. The second train also included a mess car and a mail car that was also "fitted up as a refreshment saloon." The excursion trains finally departed at noon. As soon as they were rolling, attentive waiters came through the cars serving a most festive fare.

Along the way the excursion trains made stops to impress the invited dignitaries. They admired the bridge at Elkhorn and the already completed depot buildings at Fremont. The trains traveled 91 miles to Columbus, Nebraska and the first overnight stop out on "the line" at their Camp No.1.

A Camp at Columbus
The junketeers arrived in Columbus after dark and found their camp for the night was already set up on the open land west of the station buildings.[60] The camp with a great circle of "comfortable tents was well stored with soft hay mattresses, buffalo robes and blankets." Inside a large dining tent they found food to vie with eastern hotels. As they dined a huge bonfire flared up in the moonlit night sky. Pawnee Indians from the nearby reservation staged a war dance replete with "all the wild and hideous yell, grotesque shapes and contortions that have ever been witnessed by a civilized assemblage."[61] As Pawnees savagely danced in

moonlight and dimming campfire they raised the heart rate of many pompous gentlemen and other faint-hearted guests.

Photograph by Carbutt. Courtesy Union Pacific Railroad Museum.

The Excursionists around the morning campfire.

Just before dawn the next morning the Excursionists were jolted awake by the "most unearthly whoops and yells." Mounted "savages" raced around the trains and through the camp in full war paint and battle gear. As the men quivered and ladies screamed, General Dodge hurried around the camp to calm the excited guests. He explained that they were friendly Pawnee and some of them had served under him as military scouts. A mock battle ensued and even a pseudo scalping, chilling many of the guests, until Durant tossed several hundred dollars worth of trinkets into the crowd of Pawnee causing a predictable mad scramble.[62] After the excitement subsided, the guests again boarded the train and rolled westward. Within a couple of miles the train stopped so the travelers could be photographed, admire the newly completed bridge over the Loup River, and view the valley beyond.

The trains rolled on along past Grand Island and Kearney Station, west of which the "authoritative" guests opined the land quite "worthless." (Little would they recognize the present day beautiful and productive Platte Valley.) To make up for time lost earlier in the day, the train rushed along at 45 miles an hour, ignoring the railroad's own operating rules. Unfortunately, the lead locomotive ran down a handcar with four workmen. Two men were killed and the handcar completely demolished. The Excursionists were only vaguely aware of the delay.[63] Nor were the passengers told, as they passed through Plum Creek, about the Indians' derailment and savage attack on a train there only two months earlier.

The Excursion trains rolled on in great style, fourteen more miles to the 100th Meridian at present day Cozad. The end of track was nowhere in sight. Only a lonesome wooden arch sign sitting atop two sturdy poles proclaimed the location of the Meridian. The train full of guests continued nearly thirty miles farther west of the 100th Meridian but still there was no end of the track in sight. The train finally rolled to a stop, after dark, at Milepost 279 a mile and a half west of the present day town of Maxwell.[64]

Platte City

A swarm of the railroad's employees arrived earlier that day to set up the Excursionists' Camp No. 2. A large group of tents went up, festively lighted with lanterns. There was a tent for a printing shop and a telegraph "office" so the press could telegraph their stories back east to their newspapers and keep their readers informed of this extravagant adventure. The camp was strategically located near the protective cover of Fort McPherson, five miles south of the railroad. By prearrangement a detachment of soldiers from the Fort was camped nearby to calm the Excursionists' fears of interference from the roaming bands of Indians still in the area.

Photograph by Carbutt. Courtesy Union Pacific Railroad Museum.
The Excursionists' Platte City (Camp No. 2) on the banks of the wide Platte River, 1866.

The travel day had been longer than expected. Even though a grand party tent had been set up for an extravagant meal, most of the Excursionists were exhausted and turned in for the night to the comfort and security of their rail cars. In the morning they were ready for an early start. The members of the ad hoc "Elkhorn Club," organized at the outset of the trip, lined up at dawn and marched together to the banks of the Platte River for an invigorating dip.

What a Day!
After the expected hearty breakfast, a full day's activities were laid out in detail for the Excursionists. Although some members of the "Elkhorn Club" were

obliged to leave on a special east-bound train for their official inspection duties, others went off to hunt buffalo and antelope.

Photograph by Carbutt. Courtesy Union Pacific Railroad Museum.
Excursionists posing outside the Press Tent.

Members of the press gathered together, wrote, and printed the first issue of the *Railroad Pioneer*.[65] The newspaper listed the railroad dignitaries and all of the invited guests. The *Railroad Pioneer* also carried a flowery proclamation with four great "Whereas" and eight lengthy "Resolves" thanking everyone for the fabulous junket.

The Excursion train left at 11 a.m. again seeking the ever-moving end of track. It was now 8 or 10 miles farther west. Along the way they met one of the railroad's foraging parties sent out earlier for fresh game. The foragers had been confronted by a large band of angry Indians who well outnumbered them. The Indians took the buffalo kill from the foragers and after arguing between themselves spared the hunters lives on condition that the whites stay away from their hunting grounds.

Photograph by Carbutt. Courtesy Union Pacific Railroad Museum.
The track laying crew taking a brief rest.

When the travelers finally arrived at the end of track they walked forward alongside the track workers and watched the Casements' sweating and highly organized crew. The visitors were awed as the crew dropped ties, spaced and straightened them, dragged out the twin bands of iron, and spiked down 800 feet of track in just a half an hour.[66] The crew paused briefly only once so that the official photographer, John C. Carbutt, could record the event.

After returning to Camp No. 2, now "officially" called Platte City, the guests gathered again for a sumptuous dinner. Beside each plate appeared a printed menu that listed a great array of roasted and boiled meat, game, vegetables, relishes, pastries, and fruits and, of course, an abundance of champagne and wine.

The entertainment that night was an hour-long display of fireworks. It was a most magnificent display. The night continued with a musical program by the celebrated Northwestern Band of Chicago and "lectures" by the humorists of the day.

Early the next morning (Friday, Oct 26th) the Excursionists were to head back eastward. Special Train No.1 was to leave at 7:30 a.m. with the railroad officials. (The government commissioners needed to officially finish their examination of the last 30 miles.)[67] Special Train No. 2 was to leave later and would connect with Train No. 1 at the 100th Meridian. However, just as the camp was breaking up there was a great demand for Professor Carbutt to again take photographs. After nearly two hours the junketeers finally boarded their train, a last whistle sounded, and the train got underway. As the east-bound train reached the sign at the 100th Meridian, it halted for an hour while Professor Carbutt once again assembled his equipment to memorialize this great adventure. When the photos were done and the travelers were back aboard, the train sped eastward at 30 miles per hour. Again the train overran a handcar and demolished it.[68]

Fifty miles east of the 100th Meridian, the trip was halted for a two hour visit to a vast prairie dog colony, spread out over nearly twenty-five square miles on both sides of the railroad.[69] The curious Excursionists were outdone by the curiosity of the "polite but incessantly chattering natives." Although numerous attempts were made to shoot them, they always seemed to disappear in the nick of time. Despite their efforts only one dead prairie dog was recovered. The little fellow was turned over to the cook and promptly disappeared.

Photograph by Carbutt. Courtesy Union Pacific Railroad Museum.

Track crew laying rails at the rate of two miles a day.

A Memorable Excursion

It seemed as though the entire trip was full of never-ending surprises. A little after dark, the train again stopped. Doc Durant had the prairie set on fire for a spectacular display.[70] "The flames extended in an unbroken line a distance of from fifteen to twenty miles and one end of the belt of fire was so near that we could feel the heat and distinctly hear the roaring and crackling of the devouring element, as it swept over the plains with almost railroad velocity, and shot up its forked flames into the somber smoky sky." Throughout the rail journey, Durant continued a non-stop press conference. He answered all reporters' questions with glowing accounts of the Union Pacific's accomplishments and the great potential for the land now open for development.

It was nearly 10 p.m. when the guests took their carriages to Herndon House or to the steamer "Denver." It was a long day indeed. The next morning some of the party ferried across the river to climb aboard stagecoaches from Council Bluffs to Chicago or other cities. Those who came by the steamer re-boarded the Denver at the Omaha dock and steamed down the river bound for Saint Joseph and their railroad connections there.

Photograph by Carbutt. Courtesy Union Pacific Railroad Museum.
Union Pacific Directors returning from the end of the line stopped to pose at the 100th Meridian.

The selling of the West had started in earnest. Despite the huge cost of the lengthy and extravagant excursion, Durant considered it most successful and was overjoyed with the entire event. What a memorable excursion!

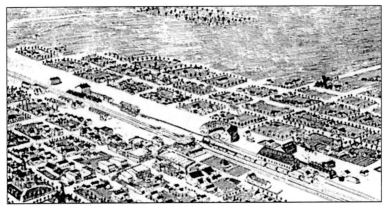

Nina Hull Miller Collection.
An Artist's Overview of Early North Platte.

9. North Platte

The confluence of the North and South Platte Rivers was a frequent stopping place for early French fur traders. Later, freighters and over 200,000 travelers from the east stopped here before they struck out westward.

The river here was wide but shallow. There were places for animals and wagons to ford and along the banks there was lush grass and numerous attractive spots for a brief rest.

Crossing the Platte

Here at the rivers' confluence the railroad location surveyors were faced with a major decision. For the railroad to follow the South Platte, the North Platte had to be crossed. It was shallow but very wide. There were shifting channels and treacherous pockets of quicksand. If the surveyors chose to follow the North Platte the entire crossing could be avoided. On the

95

other hand, by following the South Platte there were more favorable grades and a shorter route up Lodgepole Creek into Wyoming.

The railroad's surveyors chose to cross the North Platte just upstream of the rivers' confluence. Generals Dodge and Reed were not convinced of the surveyors' choice and made a special trip up the valley to look for themselves. Understandably, they were seeking a narrower channel to minimize both the bridge cost and construction time. After their first-hand look, Dodge and Reed realized the favorable grades and distance up the Lodgepole Valley made crossing the North Platte near the confluence the best choice.

The crossing would require a very long timber trestle. However, the bravado of their bridge contractor, L. B. Boomer, bolstered their confidence. The previous year Boomer had rapidly built a 1,500-foot long timber trestle for them across the Loup Forks and bridge crews were just finishing a permanent steel truss replacement bridge at the same location.

The Boomer crews were organized and ready. Within days of the decision the bridge crews moved west to the end of the track. At Kearney they loaded up their wagons, and swarmed to the North Platte crossing. During August, Boomer crews busily drove a forest of cedar piles (supplied by infamous Jack Morrow) in the sand river bottom. Row after row, the piles "marched" across the 2,300 foot wide channel.

With the Loup Forks Bridge as a pattern and suitable logs from the surrounding area, Boomer's Chicago shop busily cut and shaped the dozens of needed beams and braces. The massive timbers then went west by rail to the end of the line and were there transferred to freight wagons for the last leg of their trip.

All through September and October the bridge builders manhandled hundreds of heavy beams and stringers from the wagons into place across the tops of the piles. All this took place while they were under the continuous threat of Indian attacks.

Photograph by Arundel C. Hull.

The 2,300-foot-long bridge carried the railroad across the North Platte River, 1867.

Arthur Ferguson wrote in his diary, September 10, 1866, about the reassignment of his crew from Elm Creek to the section of the railroad line that extended west from the Platte River crossing. When the survey crew arrived at the bridge location Ferguson noted, "Here are camped some twenty-seven men of the 2nd U.S. Cavalry, also citizens enough, including our party, to make a force of nearly 70 or 80 men. In such a crowd one can sleep in comfort."[71]

Ferguson had time to reflect, "The night was dark and rainy which made the bluffs in the distance somewhat obscure, while in front the Platte could be seen like a vast plain of molten silver." The following morning, "We commenced fording the river which took the greater portion of the day.... The cavalry force also crossed the river today. The bridge forces are engaged in building a house out of sod for the use of their stock and themselves."

Ferguson's crew moved on. A second survey crew was kept busy with the bridge builders, and then set about to layout the new town of North Platte. By November, only three months after they started, the bridge crew had it ready for track crews to string out the ties and drag the rails into place. At the end of the month trains rolled over the bridge and on December 3 regular rail service commenced into the North Platte station. There was a surge of new arrivals.

The following spring the new bridge and its approaches were severely tested. The winter snow-melt and spring rain brought extraordinarily high floodwaters, but the bridge survived magnificently. Later, the Union Pacific decked it with wooden planking so it could also be used by wagons and livestock. Since the finished bridge was entirely without side protection, skittish horses and mules had to be led across. A bridge watcher was permanently stationed in a cabin near one end. He controlled the one-way traffic of animals and travelers, and after each locomotive passed over the bridge he walked its full length to check it for fire or other damage.

The Birth of a Town

Earlier when Dodge fixed the location of the river crossing, he also decided to make the south side of the river the winter terminal for construction forces and a materials supply base. More importantly, he designated the location as the next division point town. This meant permanency, and created development opportunities. Dodge had already established division points and towns at Columbus and Kearney, and he knew what was needed here. He set aside a large area of land for the railroad's sidings, shops, and other buildings. He and the other officials were "foresighted" enough to take all the property the railroads would ever need.

The surveyors laid out the town around the reserved land, prepared the maps, and recorded the surveys. The railroad land agents were close behind the surveyors and immediately started selling lots. The prices ranged from $25 to $250, one-third cash and the balance over two years. The first trader, Andrew J. Miller, arrived at North Platte November 9, on the heels of the town surveyors. He moved a building from Coldwater, Nebraska to North Platte to become the town's first citizen and businessman. The town's second building was John Burke's log cabin which he moved over from Cottonwood Springs log by log. In the following several months the new town fairly burst as excited opportunists descended on it and put up a myriad of temporary shacks and tents along with a scattering of more permanent board buildings.

The track layers added to the frenetic activity as they set up their winter quarters, but even in the face of a freezing early winter the crews continued to lay rails whenever they could. More than 2,000 toughened workmen kept on grading the roadway, dropping ties, and laying track. Before finally quitting for the winter the track layers completed seventeen more miles of rails to O'Fallon's Bluff, reaching an impressive total of 305 miles from Omaha.

Once the track crews were shut down, a large number of Casement Brothers' men were put to work building the company's station facilities. The rail boss, Jack Casement, stayed in North Platte to direct the hectic pace of construction. The men built a warehouse first, and used it for temporary housing, then finished a company bunkhouse, wash house, and mess hall. In a few short weeks they dug wells, put up a huge windmill, built a large tank, tank house, blacksmith shop, and a slaughterhouse. Then they started the most important structure of all, the roundhouse.

Jack Casement also looked out for his personal interests. He built a general store which he left in charge of a relative. To assure a high profit margin he could take advantage of the free freight on the Union Pacific. Outside the town he set up a cattle ranch to supply eating establishments with beef. He planned to bring three hundred head of good stock from Ohio, again taking advantage of free shipping on the railroad.

The pace of business was dizzying. Early in 1868 General J. H. Simpson, President of the Government Inspection Board, wrote a lengthy letter to the Editor of the *Washington Chronicle* with an extravagant description of the railroad's progress.[72] "All along the road, where the company has established its stations, settlements are springing up rapidly, and here, North

Platte Station, where three weeks ago there was nothing, are already some twenty buildings, including a brick engine roundhouse, calculated for forty engines, founded on a stone foundation, at present nearly completed for ten engines. A water tank of beautiful proportions, as they all are along the road, kept from freezing by being warmed by a stove, a frame depot of beautiful design, a large frame hotel, nearly finished to cost about $18,000, a long, spacious movable building belonging to General Casement and his brother Daniel, the great track layers of the continent, calculated for a store, eating house, and for storage purposes; together with sundry buildings."

Photograph by Arundel C. Hull.
North Platte Railroad Facilities, 1867.
This view is across Front Street toward the northwest.

101

Railroad 1869 through Nebraska

A Different Confluence

In prior years as the end of the track moved westward across Nebraska, the wagon freighters would pick up cargo at the most westerly terminal, which then became a staging stop for overland traffic. As the winter set in, bull whackers and their overland freight wagons stopped at North Platte. Here cargo built up in great piles, waiting until spring when the wagon trains could again move westward. The rough tough bull whackers were in town for the winter.

Along with the freight wagons, west-bound emigrants and Mormon caravans trudged and creaked across the three hundred miles of relatively easy-going trails up the Platte Valley. In the face of oncoming winter they became wary of moving farther and also stopped at North Platte. Hundreds of Mormons and other emigrants set up their camps around the North Platte Station. They gathered in canvas shelters on the outskirts of the town, corralled their animals, and settled down to wait for spring when they could more easily find water along the trails, and when the grass for their animals would be fresh.

In the fall the glowing publicity from the Excursionists' tour to the 100th Meridian created a flurry of excitement in the eastern papers. Once the rail service came to North Platte prospective settlers arrived at the end of the line in increasing numbers, all looking for their place in the west. Along with the serious settlers were former soldiers, perennial gold seekers, drifters, adventurers, non-conformists, n'er-do-wells, and opportunistic scam artists of every description.

Gamblers, harlots, and other camp followers who preyed on soldiers during the Civil War found them again in North Platte. Within a few weeks North Platte became the first in a progression of wild, rip-roaring railroad towns that would follow the tracks west for the next two and-a-half years.

Photograph by Russell. Courtesy Union Pacific Railroad Museum.
North Platte, Front Street, about 1868.

Added to the mix that winter were hunters and traders who roamed the open country and miners who were seeking their fortune in the desolate western hills and mountains. Even increasingly hostile Indians were driven into the town by the oncoming winter.

This polyglot of humanity and animals turned the quiet grassy plains into an eruption of frenzied activity and competition. Nowhere had there ever been such a mix. The railroad workers, graders, bridge builders and track layers, tree cutters and the like were now without pay and many of the recent arrivals were looking for some way to find grub and a place to sleep. Within a few weeks North Platte became a town of over five thousand without anyone in charge. The Army's job was to protect the railroad from the Indians; they had no legal authority over civilians. There was as yet no territorial government to create law, nor means to enforce it.

Hell-on-Wheels

The bull whackers were the hardest of the lot. They bellowed and bullied their animals when they were on the trail and they bellowed and bullied about town as they strode up and down the short main street. Without any law in town, they pretty much had their own way.

Among the earliest opportunists was a man named McDonald. His mammoth tent next to Miller's trading post commanded the attention of all arrivals with its bar and stock of liquor, the billiard tables, and gambling devices. Other sharks soon followed and with only a modicum of investment set up similar hot spots.

The Mormons pretty much stayed with their own at their camp, but most of the others in North Platte for the winter were idle for weeks at a time. The wood cutters, the graders, teamsters, and track workers were far from home and the confining influence of eastern morality. There was no one to look down their nose at them, nor wife, nor family to confine them. "What the hell," there was nothing else to spend their money on and so their main entertainment was getting drunk or gambling, either one or both and in either order. The "girls" were few. They spent their time in the saloons pushing watered drinks, urging the next bet, and making short retreats to their cribs out behind the saloon tent.

The town inhaled, and drew in nearly every gambler in the Union. Every train from the east to the end of the line was loaded with another bunch of unsavory characters looking for their chance. The sharks were brutally skillful. They fleeced the newcomers with all sorts of games. Poker was basic, but faro and keno created more excitement. Everywhere were new and exciting ways to "win a fortune." The newcomers tried their hand at "Mexican Monte" or "Chuck-a-Luck" or sudden death "Hi-Lo," but there was seldom a winner. And when there was it was usually because the dealer saw some unspent cash in the player's pocket. "Try again, my buck; nothin' like 'sperience; you are cuttin' your eye-teeth now; by and by you will be a pioneer."

Many of the newcomers had moved on west from the Civil War fights and were accustomed to rifles and revolvers. A scattering of them survived the thick of gruesome combat that left them mentally warped. Their condition didn't show on the outside but their behavior was wild and erratic. They had taken their chances with death before, and were used to it. The card dealers and barmen always had a revolver holstered on their side, as did most everyone else. A card table loser, who protested too loudly and belligerently, was likely to be shot. No big deal! No one knew his name or where he came from. Only few of the better folks were concerned enough to dig a grave for the poor fellow to see that he wasn't left out in the cold.

The taverns, gambling dens, and dance halls turned into the main engine of that winter's North Platte economy, with only a scattering of legitimate establishments: the gun stores, mercantile and grocery stores, rooming houses and eating places. The railroad gave great publicity to the few "permanent" buildings constructed, but most of the town had been thrown up in a great rush. The proprietors used a few boards of precious lumber for a false front and sign, then a timber frame to hold up the canvas tent out behind. The proprietors lived at their businesses and slept there with their revolvers at their sides. No need for a house because they would soon be moving anyway.

Photographer unknown.
Overview of North Platte about 1870.
This view is northward. The railroad shops are in the far right background.

More "refined" people began arriving in North Platte that spring and were appalled at what they saw and heard. Samuel Bowles, a pious and "upright" man from Springfield, Massachusetts was outraged when he looked at the scene and promptly gave it the immortal name "hell-on-wheels." A young medical officer passing through North Platte in May reported back home that there were 5,000 restless souls who were "having a good time gambling, drinking, and shooting each other." A hastily organized and not too effective vigilante committee provided the only law in town.

Spring Thaw

During the winter of 1867 an immense amount of snow fell across the entire west. The rivers stayed frozen until early April when heavy rains added to the melt water and triggered flooding across the entire region. No one could recall seeing the rivers so high. In many locations much of the railroad roadway was scoured away, but to Reed's relief all of the bridges, except one at Prairie Creek, withstood the floods. Luckily the North Platte Bridge, along with its earth embankment approaches, stood up against the flooding.

When the floods hit, supply trains were blocked for days. But by now the Casements had accumulated a great stockpile of ties, rails, and other materials at the North Platte supply base. When the weather finally broke crews got the spring construction started without waiting for the stream of supplies from the east. By early May they were again laying rails and making progress up the South Platte Valley. Ogallala and the Julesburg stage station were just ahead.

When the work crews left town and moved out to the end of line, a large part of North Platte population stayed on, "having a good time gambling, drinking, and shooting each other." Once train service was restored there came a rush of new arrivals. Fresh laborers by the hundreds poured in to sign on with the railroad builders and their suppliers, providing new customers for the "business men." They were greeted by several "permanent" town buildings completed during the winter: a hotel, three groceries, fifteen houses, a billiard room, and nine eating houses or drinking saloons. Of course, there remained the many false front tent buildings.

Newspaperman Stanley arrived after a fifteen-hour journey from Omaha. He noted large piles of freight along the track, beyond which there was an encampment of more than 1,200 covered wagons of the Utah-bound Mormon emigrants and other settlers heading for Idaho or Montana. "The prairie around seemed turned into a canvas city," he marveled. But as he walked past the Mormon Camp and into the short main street, his breath was taken away. "Every gambler in the Union seems to have steered his course for North Platte."[73]

Spring became a very busy season as wagon trains organized into manageable trains of twenty or thirty, with provisions and escorts arranged. The early wagons left before the ground dried out, leaving rutted trails that deepened into mud wallows with each following wagon. Travelers with the early wagon trains hunted game along the way, but with each passing week the game was driven farther and farther away angering the Indian tribes and reducing the food supply for the following wagon trains.

For rail travelers, finding overnight accommodations in North Platte was nigh impossible. Episcopal Bishop D. S. Tuttle came through on a journey west and asked that his party be lodged in the hotel (which was owned by Reed and his wife Jenny). It was full, but after a bit of commotion they succeeded in finding a room for the two women in the party, forcing the Bishop to sleep with his male companions under blankets on the floor of a common room. The next morning, after Reed made their acquaintance, he arranged for his party to ride on a flat car in one of the west-bound construction trains thus saving them miles of stagecoach travel and exposure to Indians. Before he left, Bishop Tuttle conducted a Whitsunday service in the Reeds' room. He wrote, "I read the morning service entire except the lesson and commandments and we commended ourselves especially to the protection of the Heavenly Father."[74]

By May the tracks reached Ogallala. In June they reached the old stage station of Julesburg. When it became the next materials supply base, the gamblers and their compatriots moved on to Julesburg. Almost overnight North Platte shrank from five thousand to a few hundred. The pattern was set for the rolling "hell-on-wheels" towns that would pick up and move westward every few weeks until the railroads met at Promontory.

Afterglow

In June of 1867 when photographer, Arundel Hull, arrived at North Platte, he found railroad shops and an impressive large brick roundhouse under construction. A group of Sioux Indians camped out nearby were giving the townspeople great anxiety since only a few months earlier the Sioux had ruthlessly attacked the early whites. Hull apparently persuaded the Indians to let him take photographs. He gave some photographs to them and sold a good many prints around town, helping to fund his further travels. The following year while returning from a trip with William Jackson, Hull again photographed the railroad shops and the finished roundhouse. He heard how the shops had scarcely been completed when the threat of Indian attack sent the townspeople scurrying for protection. On frequent occasions the sturdily built roundhouse was the safest refuge in time of danger.

Photograph by Arundel C. Hull.

Sioux Teepees on the plains near North Platte, 1868.

North Platte shops became a boon to the settlers in another quite special way. An accommodating engineer rigged up a bathhouse in one of the shops where towns-people were free to enjoy hot or cold baths. The settlers who took advantage of that privilege would not have agreed with the historian who said, "The railroad shops cost $300,000 but were not worth three cents to the railroad. They were merely one of the many requirements of the government that greatly increased costs of building the road."

It was at North Platte that Hull first saw *The Frontier Index,* popularly called the "newspaper-on-wheels." Brothers Fred and Leigh Freeman had bought the newspaper at Fort Kearny and periodically moved it westward to keep it near the head of the railroad construction. It gave a frank picture of life in the new towns, and progress of the railroad was reported week by week. Frequent deaths were given no more attention than any other news item. The Freemans published only a few issues of the *Index* at North Platte and within weeks they moved the newspaper on to the next rail-head at Julesburg.

In 1884 (some seven years after the rail construction passed through), travelers found North Platte to be a thriving city. The travel guide of the day, *The Pacific Tourist,* described the town:

> *"It is a thriving city and outside of Omaha, has the most extensive machine and repair shops on the line of the road. The roundhouse has twenty stalls and it together with the machine and repair shops are substantially built of brick. In these shops engines and cars are either*

111

*repaired or entirely built over and render them
as good as new.*

*"The town has about 2,000 inhabitants having
steadily grown from the few hundred who
stayed behind when the construction rolled on in
1867. There are two wide awake newspapers,
the Republican, being a weekly and the Western
Nebraskian being a semi-weekly. The Railroad
House is the largest and leading hotel. About
150 men are given constant employment at the
shops.*

*"There are also one or two companies of troops
stationed here, not to protect the railroad from
the savages, since that necessity has passed,
but for economy in keeping troops on frontier
duty.*

*"The town also has two or three church
edifices, a brick courthouse and a brick
schoolhouse, both new and presenting a fine
appearance. There are also several elegant
private residences. The bluffs are in near
view, both north and south, and give quite a
picturesque appearance to the country and
immediate vicinity."*[75]

The Infamous Jack Morrow

Jack Morrow spent his early years as a teamster along
many of the emigrant trails. During these years he
became familiar with much of the terrain across the
west and was always searching for "opportunities." One
of the "opportunities" was a spot on the Oregon Trail
near the Platte River junction. There he set up his

Junction Ranch and trading post. His unsavory reputation soon spread up and down the trail as emigrants told of various misfortunes they encountered as they approached the trading post. Frequently the wagon trains lost livestock, the animals run off by marauding "Indians." Then as wagon trains approached the Junction Ranch they encountered "the ditch." Morrow dug a ditch and threw up a dike across the flat valley bottom. The ditch was purposely too wide and too deep for heavy freight wagons and prairie schooners to cross and they were forced to travel directly through his trading post. Under pressure, travelers replenished supplies from his ample stock of firearms, clothing, and other provisions, always at outrageous prices. The dance hall and the liquor supply were hard to pass up for some travelers.

At the trading post Jack Morrow, sporting a diamond stick pin in a dirty shirt, would be disarmingly sympathetic about their livestock losses and offer to sell them animals from his own herd, at a high price of course, "just to help them out."[76] A few weeks later the stolen animals were often "found" in the nearby canyons and sold to other emigrants.

Photograph by Arundel C. Hull.
Infamous "Jack" Morrow, 1869.

Railroad 1869 through Nebraska

The Morrow ranch lay near Moran Canyon where there was a large stand of cedar trees. Although he did not own the land he did not hesitate to cut timber there for his own ranch buildings. When the railroad surveyors crossed Nebraska in 1866, Morrow spotted another opportunity. He set up a logging operation in the canyon where he cut the timber and produced ties and telegraph poles to sell to the railroad. His reputation and his rough crew of Indians and squaw men dissuaded anyone from challenging him. He knew where there were other good stands of timber, and over the next three years he supplied hundreds of thousands of ties and cordwood for fuel, "following the market" as the railroad moved across Wyoming.

Morrow and his unsavory followers were not above outright robbery. In the fall of 1868 robbers held up a stagecoach in which young photographer Arundel Hull was riding. Hull pleaded with the robbers not to take his photographic equipment since it was his means of livelihood. Persuaded, the leader demanded a promise that Hull take photographs of him the next time they met. Hull later took photographs of Jack Morrow at both Benton and Green River, Wyoming.[77]

In an interesting twist of history, when Arundel Hull married he discovered from his new wife that several years earlier, in 1860, her family had lost a herd of horses when their wagon train passed near the Junction Ranch.[78]

To some Morrow was a colorful, eccentric braggart. To most of those travelers who encountered him he was an exploiter and common thief.

Photograph by Eugene Arundel Miller.

Old Town Ogallala, 2004.

10. Ogallala

Before Union Pacific construction crews surged across the plains, the only settlements in the area were cattle ranches on the emigrant and freight wagon roads. As the ranches emerged into stage stations, mail drops, and telegraph stations, numerous skirmishes took place as the Indians resisted the white man's incursion into their traditional lands.

After one encounter the Indian attackers retreated to a nearby bluff, out of range of the soldiers' weapons, they thought. They turned their backs on the soldiers and "indulged in many taunting and inelegant gestures The display was soon brought to a close by a well-directed volley of rifle shots which caused the Indians to fly in disorder."[79]

The Advance Crews

In the fall of 1866 as the Casements were setting up their winter supply base at North Platte, surveyors and other work crews were many miles west. The location surveyors were in Wyoming fixing the route location. A second wave of surveyor crews was in western Nebraska staking out the work for the several grading crews and bridge builders.

Arthur Ferguson's diary for October 1866 told of working in the vicinity of Alkali, present day Paxton. His survey crew cut saplings along the river to make hundreds of stakes, and they set the prairie on fire so they could see their survey lines and stakes. He wrote of a few days of pleasant weather then reported a violent gale and pouring rain, bleak and dismal, damp, cold, and windy. One morning Ferguson's tent was blown down and he struggled unsuccessfully to get it set up and staked down again. He could do nothing but huddle in the storm and wait it out. Even as the surveyors moved west so did the violent weather. Then, adding to their anxiety, wolves circled their camp at night and howled incessantly.

The surveyors usually set up their camp near to the graders' camp for additional protection against the Indians. For the most part, however, the surveyors and graders were well west of the main construction forces and had scant real protection against Indian raids. In one night time foray the Indians swept out of the hills and drove off eighty head of cattle, the grading crews' entire traveling meat supply. Then there were the toughs from the graders' camp itself. One night someone from the grading crew made off with four mules and two saddles. Soon after, graders reported a drunken quarrel and a murder.

Ferguson's diary for mid-November records a terrific snow storm, "howling, moaning, and shrieking" and he describes awaking to find snow all about, even a foot of snow on their bedding. "The river in front is madly hissing and foaming by, almost choked up with floating ice, huge masses of which crushed together, heaving upwards layer upon layer only to be hurled down and carried onward by the surging waters of the Platte."80

In the face of the weather and their heightened fear of the "bloody, vengeful, scalping knife of the savage," men from the grading crews started to leave camp and make their way back along the line to "civilization." The surveyors likewise started east, loading their gear on wagons, heading to the end of the track where they could catch a rail ride back to Omaha.81

Indians Again
In the spring of 1867 there were huge piles of ties, rails, and other supplies at North Platte. When the crews started up, the end of the track was only a few miles away from the materials base. Jack Casement's track layer crews quickly built up their momentum, and by May 27 the track laying crews were moving at an impressive pace, over and over dragging the two strips of heavy steel rails across the ties and rhythmically spiking them down: one spike, each rail, each tie.

Anxious to get official approval of the line so far and to get the government bonds released, Dodge brought the government commissioners out along the line to inspect the work. At midday the work crews and inspection party stopped just past present day Ogallala and stacked their rifles. As they settled into a relaxed lunchtime mood, a hundred Sioux Indians burst out of a small ravine off to the side of the track. The raiders went after the mules and horses grazing nearby, cut several animals out of the herd, and got away before the workers could even unstack their rifles. The three commissioners and Dodge were "men of action" and ran to Dodge's rail car for firearms to help drive off the Indians. The Sioux, however, were after only the mules and horses and weren't yet ready to take on the white men. After their lightning raid the Indians raced off as fast as they came. The entire raid seemed to take only seconds.

Capt. Luther North's Company of Pawnee Scouts was nearby at the end of track. The troops quickly pursued the Sioux and in a few miles overtook the raiders. The captured mules slowed the Sioux so they abandoned them and continued to flee. In the running fight one of the raiding Sioux had his horse shot out from under him. One of the Pawnee Scouts, Baptiste Behale, quickly dismounted, ran up close to the Sioux, and let fly an arrow into the raider's right side. The arrow had such force that the point came out his left side. The wounded Sioux staggered, then grabbed at the arrow and pulled it the rest of the way through his body. He fitted it into his own bow and sent it back at Baptiste, narrowly missing him! The wounded brave took only a couple more steps, and then fell dead. It was a close call for Baptiste.

The raid was only one of many Sioux attacks that spring and it wouldn't be the last. Dodge was highly agitated about the persistent raids and lost his temper. "We've got to clean the damn Indians out or give up building the Union Pacific Railroad. The government has to make a choice."

Photographer Unknown. Courtesy Goodall City Library.
The Aufdengarten Stores, Ogallala.

A Cattle Town

In the spring of 1867 a few North Platte drifters made their way to the new town of Ogallala, where they swaggered about town unimpeded. After the rails reached the station in May 1867, the town became a shipping point for cattle driven up from Texas. Cattlemen from Texas found Ogallala a good location for their headquarters. There were large areas of prairie grass nearby and plenty of water at the river. The cattlemen were a tough bunch also. They tangled with the railroad hangers-on at their very first meeting, and started a continuing series of fights and brawls. Soon a few transient bull whackers entered the mix of toughs, and the town quickly earned a reputation as a rough place, nowhere to be unless you were prepared to fight. It was a wild town with restless people, referred to as the "Gomorrah of the Plains."[82]

Later the bull whackers and many of the railroad toughs moved on, but the cattlemen stayed and Ogallala grew as a great cattle-shipping point. In later years vast herds of Longhorns were driven up from Texas to be loaded at Ogallala and shipped back east or up north to the Indian agencies. By 1880 over 50,000 head of cattle were being driven up each year.

Soon after the tracks passed through Ogallala, the railroad built side tracks, started a depot, and built a water tank. However, there was little growth for the next few years. The first "store" was a trading post run from an earth dugout south of the railroad. The proprietor, Louis Aufdengarten, soon expanded to a new frame building and signaled the real beginning of the town.[83] Over the next few years the town boasted of the new Aufdengarten store, two boarding houses, and of course, a saloon.[84] Soon the railroad built a cattle-loading chute and triggered a surge of activity.

Hull's Trips
On his first trip out along the railroad in 1867 photographer Arundel Hull arrived in Ogallala to see the start of a depot building and a scattering of other structures. It was indeed the wildest town Hull had yet seen. There was not much to photograph and virtually no customers. None of the cattlemen or rail workers were interested in photographs and the remaining few, who were trying to make Ogallala a home, had no money to spend.

At Ogallala, Hull was close to the end of train travel. He could go on to Julesburg, Sidney, and Pine Bluffs by rail but beyond Pine Bluffs he had to take a stagecoach. He chose to head south to the Colorado gold country for the winter. The following year he returned again and stopped momentarily at Ogallala. Settlers had begun to arrive but there was still a dearth of photograph customers.

Photograph by Arundel C. Hull.
Sod House in Ogallala, 1867.
A scattering of tents, at the right, housed less permanent residents.

Boot Hill

Early in 1867 the Sioux attacked a work train killing three track layers. The track layers may possibly be the first occupants of the cemetery at the north edge of Ogallala later called "Boot Hill." This cemetery seemed to have a steady flow of customers. Trivial incidents frequently ended in a confrontation and with someone dead. One of the many local legends tells of a man killed because he insulted two brothers by calling them "Yankee Bean Eaters."[85] Rattlesnake Ed was killed over a nine dollar bet during a Monte game. Another gambler met his fate by simply questioning a winning poker hand, and others demised during drunken shoot outs at the Cowboy Rest Saloon.

Often the victims were known only by a nickname, but sometimes they were totally unknown. They ended up buried in a shallow grave in a canvas sack, fully clothed and with their boots on. Sometimes a wooden board marked the grave. Boot Hill became the final resting place of gamblers, soldiers who re-fought the Civil War in a barroom, horse thieves, and others who ran afoul of the sheriff. In the decade or two following the arrival of the Union Pacific, more than a hundred people were laid in shallow graves on Boot Hill . . . remarkable for a settlement whose population never exceeded 130.

Boot Hill Cemetery, Ogallala.

A Bull Whacker

A bull whacker was one of the most colorful characters in the frontier west. He had to be unusually strong to handle eight or ten yoke of oxen hitched to two large unwieldy freight wagons. The bull whacker was usually large, had long unkempt hair and a dirty beard. His phenomenal oath and his nasty whip were his tools. The whip with its three-foot-long handle controlled a braided rawhide lash seldom less than twenty feet long ending with a ribboned thong. This persuader made quite an impression on the ox-teams, driving them at the magic rate of twenty miles per day. When a lazy ox received a reminder from the whip it was as though he had been seared with a red-hot iron.

Bull whackers took great pride in their astonishing accuracy with the lash. A favorite pastime was to set a coin on the top of a stick stuck in the ground some fifteen or twenty feet away. If a braggart knocked the coin off without touching the stake, the money was his. If the stake is disturbed, the thrower lost it. One story tells of a bull whacker who a bet a comrade a pint of whiskey that he could cut the cloth on the back of his pants without touching the skin. The comrade stooped over in position to give fair chance. The lash was delivered but not with the accuracy expected, resulting in the "tallest jump ever put on record." The comrade was missing a portion of his skin, as well as a large portion of his breeches, but the bull whacker's cry was even more plaintive, "Thunder, I've lost my whiskey."

Railroad 1869 through Nebraska

Bull whackers were among the best swearers in the country. His profanity often exceeded that of the mates aboard a Mississippi River Packet, with "some of the most astounding oaths that ever fell on the ear." General Sherman wrote, "One of the members of a freighting firm in Saint Louis desired to discourage the continual blasphemy of the bull whackers in their employ. Orders were issued to their train-masters to discharge any man that should curse the cattle. The new wagon-masters were selected more for their piety than for any extensive knowledge of their duties in the handling of trains. Their outfit had not proceeded more than a hundred fifty miles before it was stuck fast. A messenger was dispatched to the firm with information that the cattle would not pull a pound unless they were cursed as usual. Permission was granted, after which the train proceeded to Salt Lake to which place good time was made."

Lithograph by William H. Jackson.
Courtesy Scotts Bluff National Monument.

**Wagon trains crossing the South Platte River 1866,
near present day Julesburg.**

11. Four Julesburgs

During the 1850s and 60s thousands of travelers trekked westward along the South Platte River. Most crossed the sandy channel opposite the mouth of Lodgepole Creek, then followed the creek into Wyoming. When gold was discovered in Colorado a good many travelers continued along the South Platte into Colorado and the gold country.

The junction of Lodgepole Creek and the South Platte River proved to be an advantageous spot for a trading post. For several years before the arrival of the railroad, the owner, Jules Beni (also known as Jules

Reni, Rene Benoit, Rene Jules, and other aliases) fully exploited the location and his monopoly. Beni bullied and cheated both travelers and settlers alike. [86]

Bad from the Start

When the Overland Stage Company's line was set up, Beni's trading post was also a natural location for one of the home stations. Those stations were typically located about 50 miles apart. They usually consisted of a ranch house, stable, and a cluster of other small sheds and shacks. They were staffed by a station master and several other workers. They offered the travelers meals and rudimentary overnight accommodations, and sold liquor and other supplies at highly inflated prices.

About every fifteen miles in between home stations were swing stations. These primitive affairs were little more than hovels staffed by a single occupant. They were for only a brief stop and a place for the stage drivers to "swing" fresh horses into their teams.

Being unprotected, the swing stations, and even home stations, were frequently targeted by Indian raiding parties. The raiders stole horses and burned both buildings and hay. To discourage the persistent raiders the stage line owners dispatched one of their toughest men, Jack Slade, to "send a message." Slade set out for Julesburg to meet with four other Overland company men to track down and punish the Indian raiders. When Slade arrived in Julesburg he sized up Jules Beni and judged him to be untrustworthy and a dangerous liar. The two took an instant dislike of each other. That grew into a hatred that lasted the rest of their lives.[87]

Slade and his posse rode out across the countryside and successfully tracked down the Indian raiders. In a short gun battle they killed three of them, wounded two, and captured four. In no time at all Slade shot their leader and hung all the rest, both the captured and the wounded. He left them hanging "as a message."[88]

In 1860 Indian raids against the stage line stopped, but other troubles persisted. At swing stations supplies and horses continued to be stolen and stagecoaches held up. The robbers seemed to know all about valuable shipments and rich travelers. The Overland owners again sent their top "trouble-shooter" (what an apt moniker for a gunman) to Julesburg. He was to do whatever was needed to solve the robbery problem.

Slade arrived in town and after talking to the townspeople and looking about for three days decided Beni was behind it all.[89] Slade openly declared Beni to be a liar and crook. Beni was infuriated when he got wind of the insult, grabbed a shotgun and set off to search for Slade. Beni caught Slade by surprise and blasted him with both barrels. Hitting him in the chest, he reloaded, shot him in the back, reloaded, shot him a third time, and left him to die. The townspeople were aghast. They seized Beni and prepared to hang him from a nearby telegraph pole. The Overland Stage Company president arrived at that very moment and intervened, extracting Beni's promise to leave town and never come back.[90]

Slade, injured by multiple shot gun blasts, was carried back to the station. There a doctor worked on him for several hours digging out shot-gun pellets, and a priest administered last rites. The stage line owners put him on an east-bound stage to get to better medical facilities, fully expecting him to die along the way. But Slade refused to die. After an agonizing seventeen-day, 800 mile, bone jarring stage journey, he was delivered to a Saint Louis hospital. With sheer will power and bitter determination he spent the better part of the next year recovering. Now, nothing was going to keep him from avenging Jules Beni's cowardly act.

Months later when Slade finally left the hospital he headed west. He first visited the officer-in-charge at Fort Laramie. There he received tacit approval to hunt down Beni and extract "justice." Even though months earlier Beni promised to leave the area, he had made no move to do so. It wasn't long before Slade and four trusted sidekicks were on his trail. At a swing station in the corner of Colorado, Slade learned that Beni had been there only a couple of hours earlier. Being unable to ride hard, Slade sent his trusted sideriders racing on ahead to capture him.

When Slade arrived at the next station he found Beni tied to the corral fence. Slade alternatively swigged down whiskey and shot various parts off Beni: hand, arm, shoulder, thigh...all the time telling him of the months of agony he went through after their last encounter. Beni passed out, three times. Each time Slade sloshed a bucked of cold water over his head to bring him back around. As Slade's gruesome revenge unfolded, three stagecoaches arrived for a short stop but the passengers stayed on to witness the personal carnage. Over 24 hours Slade squeezed off twenty-two shots, then in one final spasm squeezed off a round directly into Beni's mouth. Unmoved by his own bloody drama, Slade unsheathed his Bowie knife, cut the rope that held Beni to the fence, and neatly sliced off both of the dead man's ears. He shoved the ears in his pocket, took a long draught of whiskey, and staggered into the station.[91]

Slade's fearsome reputation became even more widespread and in ensuing years he frequently reinforced it in and out of Julesburg. His increasing outbursts of viciousness, relentless pursuit, and his cold murder of anyone who crossed him could no longer be tolerated by the stage line. In the spring of 1862, after much trepidation, the company officials finally relieved him of his duties. He took the news with surprising calm and moved to Montana, where, despite his efforts to become a peaceful citizen, his violent past caught up with him. There the local vigilante committee wrote the final chapter to Jack Slade's "earie" tale.

Indians Everywhere

By the mid-1860s Julesburg had a "reputation." It was more than just a hamlet. There were settlers and traders, with a stage station busy with traffic to the Colorado gold fields. But the collection of tents and wood shanties were located on traditional Indian trails and fully exposed to the resentful natives.

In October 1864, a small contingent of soldiers were sent from Fort Laramie to establish a fort at Julesburg from which to protect the South Platte Valley from the increasing attacks by Cheyenne Indians. When Captain O'Brien and his small group of troopers arrived at the Julesburg trading post they found virtually nothing they could use to build the fort. Timber was miles away. In fact, there wasn't even much brush along the rivers.

They dug rifle pits, pitched their tents near the stage station, and set up their camp. As winter approached, Captain O'Brien purchased a ranch with a sod house about a mile west.[92] With timber hauled in from Jack Morrow's place near the Platte River junction a log fort soon began taking shape. A five-foot-high sod fence went up to encircle the HQ building, barracks, and stables.[93] By the end of the year Camp Rankin, later to be renamed Fort Sedgwick, was completed.

It was none too soon. Earlier that fall a blundering Colorado Volunteer Col. Chivington and his soldiers attacked a peaceful Indian encampment to the south on Sand Creek. In their rampage they killed 200 Cheyenne Indians, mostly women, children, and old people.[94] The murderous attack outraged the Indians throughout the prairie and unleashed a coalition of Cheyenne, Sioux, and Arapahoe warriors in series of bloody retaliatory raids on settlements and travelers.

In January 1865 the outraged Indians attacked a wagon train four miles east of Camp Rankin, luring a detachment of soldiers into a force of over a thousand warriors. The soldiers retreated back into the new Fort in a chaotic race past the Julesburg village. The Indians decimated the wagon train, destroying sacks of U.S. Mail, express packages, and bundles of Treasury Notes. At the village they smashed windows and doors, set buildings afire, and left Julesburg in smoky ruins. Five civilians and fifteen soldiers were dead on the frozen prairie.[95] Jack Morrow, who happened to be at the Fort, rushed out with the soldiers to defend the town and fort. He was greatly praised for his bravery.

Photograph by Phyllis Forsling Miller.

Julesburg Number One, Marker and Reader Board, 2003.

About a month after the attack a detachment of soldiers was sent from Camp Rankin to Alkali (present day Paxton) to pick up a howitzer.[96] They returned along with one of the stages only to look down on 1,200 warriors swirling around the partially rebuilt Julesburg looting, ransacking, and setting it afire. At the Fort the fifteen soldiers remaining there, and fifty civilians who fled to the Fort for protection, repelled the Indians' attempts to overwhelm it. The returning soldiers and stage dashed through the startled Indians to the relative safety of the sod walls of the Fort. By late afternoon the Indians' destruction of the village was complete. The warriors withdrew to the north side of the river where they threw up a constant din celebrating through the night. Before daylight the following morning the Indians dispersed out onto the Plains. A late morning scouting party found most telegraph poles gone and the lines down as far as they could see.

Later that year Camp Rankin became "permanent" and was renamed Fort Sedgwick, as the Army was convinced it was crucial to the control of the frontier. Along with the new status was the declaration of the surrounding area as a military reservation, important only in that no liquor was allowed.

Julesburg Number Two
In the spring of 1866, predictably, a new Julesburg was established just outside the military reservation, four miles east of the post. The second Julesburg consisted of the stage station, an obligatory saloon, blacksmith shop, a store, and a couple of warehouses. It was little more than a hamlet, too far from the Fort for protection and under the continuing threat of Indian attack.

Meanwhile back at the Fort, a series of incompetent officers reassigned from Civil War duty and soldiers anxious to be discharged were assigned to this desolate outpost. Trouble boiled with reports of payoffs, kick backs, and illegal liquor. In 1866 a prairie fire threatened to sweep through the Fort, but was narrowly averted by a last minute backfire. There was no provision for fire protection except for a few barrels of water and leather buckets. Only a few months later a fire burned the stables to the ground and killed 39 horses.

Finally, the Railroad
The railroad location surveyors had taken advantage of those gentle grades along the Platte River all the way from Omaha to the Platte River junction. As the terrain steepened in western Nebraska the surveyors explored several routes, examining grades and distances for the best way to cross the Rocky Mountains. They settled on

a route that followed the South Platte River to Julesburg and then up Lodgepole Creek into Wyoming.

Since the location surveyors worked many miles ahead of the actual rail construction, they had almost no protection from Indian raids. The forts were widely spaced and the soldiers were always a considerable distance away. As the surveyors moved west from North Platte and Ogallala, they became increasingly exposed to harassment by the Indians.

The grading crews were likewise exposed. In the spring of 1867 the Casements and their subcontractors' 2,000 graders, spread out for many miles along the line. Early in May a large grading crew was working a few miles east of the Julesburg stage station when an Indian raiding party burst over a nearby ridge. They drove off all of the contractors' livestock, their horses and mules, and the cattle, their fresh meat supply. The graders hi-tailed it back several miles to the relative safety of the work train at the end of line. When Dodge learned of the raid he telegraphed General Sherman, who had command of the Army in the West, "They scared the workman out of their boots, so they abandoned the work and we cannot get them back."[97]

When Sherman arrived at Fort Sedgwick to look over the situation he found that, "the Indians are everywhere." As if to confirm his assessment, a few days later a party of about fifty Cheyenne galloped directly into the stage station. The settlers were alert enough to meet them with their own gunfire. However, the settlers were badly outnumbered. The shooting and war whoops could be heard inside the stockade at Fort Sedgwick.

The cavalrymen stationed there immediately mounted up and raced to the town to drive off the attackers. Major Henry Parry followed the other soldiers to the town to look after the wounded. He treated five men who had been hit with arrows. "I never saw an arrow wound before and regard them as worse than a bullet wound." In the fracas two of the settlers had been killed, scalped, and mutilated. Major Parry later wrote about the gruesome sight that was left when the raiding party fled: "One of the men killed was lying on the ground pinned to the earth by an arrow through his neck. He must have been shot after he had been scalped."

Sinful Julesburg (Number Three)

On June 24 the Casements' rail layers rolled across the corner of Colorado without a break in their pace. Where the rails left the South Platte and turned to go up Lodgepole Creek they set up Julesburg Station on the north side of the river, a third Julesburg. At first the town was only a collection of tents and shanties clustered around the railroad station. It had a population of forty men and one woman. Many of them were settlers who moved over from the south side of the Platte River to gain better protection from the Indians. Little did they realize they were about to be overwhelmed by outlaws of another kind.

Back in North Platte the word passed around that Julesburg was to be the next supply base. That meant that the crews and work trains were moving up from their winter headquarters at North Platte. Almost overnight the "sharpers" and their henchmen moved enmass to keep up with their "customers." North Platte shrank from several thousand people to only 300 in a matter of a few week.

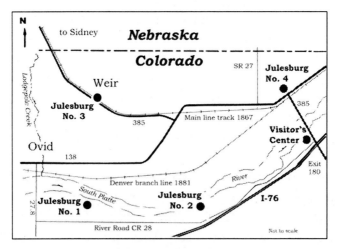

Four Julesburgs.

The unsavory traders, gamblers, whiskey merchants, prostitutes and all their retinue moved into Julesburg feed off the rail crews, tie cutters and teamsters, the soldiers, and any and all that might pass through this new town. By the end of July the settlement at Julesburg swelled into a boomtown of 4,000 people, some wild claims were as high as 7,000.

A profusion of gambling houses, saloons, and other "businesses" lined up along main street in a sea of canvas tents, shanties of boards stuck in the ground, and sod hovels spreading out onto the plains. Near the station house and railroad yards a few more substantial buildings were put up: a hotel and eating houses and a so called "theater." One visitor reported that of the 1,200 buildings in town at least 900 were dedicated to some sort of vice.[98]

On the main street the "Big Tent" seemed to be one of the main centers of action. It was forty feet wide and a hundred feet long and had a board floor. Down one side of the tent was a long bar with mirrors and pictures, glassware, and a wide selection of liquors and cigars. Gambling tables surrounded the dance floor and a band played – day and night – to keep the money coming in. All this was splendidly helped along by strumpets in light and airy frocks, who pushed for drinks, dances, and time in the cribs out behind.

The con-men moved aggressively to cash in on the free-spending railroad workers when they got a few hours time in town. They watched for a flash of cash when workers left the railroad paymaster, and were determined to separate them from their pay. "Double your money, fast," was the cry from the barkers outside the gambling tents. If that didn't move the gullible, then cheap whiskey, or even free drinks, helped them loosen up. If the card sharks didn't get all their money, strong-armed thugs simply robbed them openly – day or night, it made no difference.

The women were described as "expensive articles" and accounted for a large part of the money trading hands. They pranced down the main street carrying fancy derringers slung to their waists. They were "dangerously expert" with those small weapons. If they "got into a fuss" they had no need to call on western chivalry. With their derringer they would not be abused by any man, even the one they may have just robbed.

General Augur and his staff came to inspect the railroad progress but they were eager also to see the "sights." Construction Engineer Reed, being somewhat prudish, excused himself but arranged for the tough contractor Dan Casement to be their guide. Dan was not a stranger to the "street" and knew his way around. First, he took them to a dance hall whose owners boasted about their newly arrived "ladies" from whom incredulous visitors witnessed profanity and indecency "that would disgust a more hardened person than I." They moved on to a bigger gambling house where the visitors saw drunken workmen blowing their week's earnings on a few hands of cards or a couple throw of the dice. There the "ladies" clung to their reeling companions, egging them on while they picked their pockets. When the visitors tired of the sport in one house, Dan led them on to other establishments where the same scenes were repeated. At last they came to the theater and were invited to a peek at the girls.

The "Newspaper-on-Wheels"
In the spring of 1867 Leigh Freeman and his brother Fred continued to publish *The Frontier Index* in North Platte but as the rails reached Julesburg their North Platte subscribers and advertisers disappeared virtually overnight. The best thing to do was to follow the crowd.

By July *The Frontier Index* was up and ready for their eight month run at Julesburg. In their July 26 issue they apologized to their readers. *"The Index* is one day behind time, on account of waiting for our paper to come, but we were at last disappointed and compelled to issue on brown paper."[99]

The editors tuned into everything of local interest, as was reflected in various news items; "The UPRR is laying over two miles of track per day and will soon average three miles per day." "A large rattlesnake with eighteen rattles was killed...three men were killed by Indians..." "The UPRR is erecting a splendid passenger depot at this station which will be completed within the next ten days." "Nearly one hundred wagon loads of pine lumber reached this point from Denver yesterday morning."

Four Julesburgs

The Freemans also frequently displayed their sense of humor in print. "The weather has been so hot for the past week that the thermometer had to be lengthened for the mercury to run up. It has ranged from 120 to 126 in the shade.".

Even though the railroad moved rapidly westward in the summer and fall of 1867, *The Frontier Index* remained in Julesburg through the winter. The Freeman Brothers again watched the population exodus and finally picked up to move the following March.

In August a fellow newspaper man, reporter Henry M. Stanley, visited *The Frontier Index* to see for himself "sinful Julesburg." At first he was favorably impressed. He found a comfortable hotel filled with well-dressed guests. "Everybody had gold watches attached to expensive chains, and several wore patent leather boots. I thought they were all great capitalists, but was astonished to find they were only clerks, ticket agents, conductors, engineers... I walked on till I came to a dance-house, bearing the euphonious title of "King of the Hills" gorgeously decorated and brilliantly lighted. The ground floor was as crowded as it could well be, and all were talking loud and fast and mostly everyone seemed bent on debauchery and dissipation. The women appeared to be the most reckless and the men seemed nothing loath to enter a whirlpool of sin. The managers of the saloons rake in greenbacks by hundreds every night; there appears to be plenty of money here, and plenty of fools to squander it." There was no semblance of town organization or authority. The soldiers at nearby Fort Sedgwick were there to protect the workmen from Indian raids not to provide a local police force. In town there was no law. Reed called it, "A place where vice and crime stalk unblushingly in the midday sun." There were men who would murder for five dollars – and think nothing of it. There were no consequences except the risk from the next man who might also want the five. Not a day passed without a dead body stretched out somewhere, pockets turned inside out. The townspeople were strangely indifferent, or maybe resigned that there was "no point in protesting."

Claim Jumpers

The problems grew out of the railroad's way of doing business. As soon as the railroad's surveyors laid out the town, the lots were sold off by the railroad land agent on the spot. The railroad badly needed cash and the agent and his bosses could get a slice of the cash as it passed through their hands. There was intense competition for the largest and best locations and that inevitably led to double-dealing. Corruption and bribery became commonplace.

The tough saloon operators became so brazen that they ignored the formality of property ownership or property lines. It mattered not to the con-men. They grabbed their location along Main Street simply by occupancy then put up their buildings wherever they wanted "first come first served." The railroad's land agent was outraged but powerless to stand up against the saloon men and their toughs. When the agent telegraphed General Dodge to report the problem, the General became furious. Gambling, drinking, and prostitution was one thing but "claim jumping" the company land was quite another.

Dodge wired back to Jack Casement to have his men

clean up the town and hold the gamblers until they paid for their lots. He knew that Jack Casement would take on the task with great verve and he didn't bother with specific instructions. Jack Casement rounded up 200 men from his work crews, most of them former soldiers, armed them with rifles from the work train, and marched into town for a face to face with the gamblers. The gamblers, tough and used to bluffing their way, spat in Jack's face. They hadn't really appreciated that Jack would "out-tough" them. With deliberate calm he ordered his men to open fire; he didn't care who was hit or how many. Facing the fusillade some of the belligerent crowd were killed, others immediately lost their toughness altogether, and the rest of them fled into the prairie. Those who fled sent word back that they would willingly pay for their lots.

Later Dodge arrived and saw the problem had been solved. When he asked Jack what happened Jack led Dodge a short distance to the edge of town where there were several fresh graves, "General, they all died in their boots and Julesburg has been quiet since." There were no lawmen. When Casement cleaned up Julesburg, he did so without any authority whatsoever; he simply had more men and more guns than the others. The railroad asked for martial law but the soldiers weren't about to take on the role of local constables.

West Along the Line
As the track crews moved through the corner of Colorado the location surveyors were miles to the west. Next in the procession were the construction surveyors, setting out stakes for embankments and bridges.

While they were camped at Fort Sedgewick Arthur Ferguson noted in his diary the surveyors heard reports of Indian attacks. In early June as they were working up Lodgepole Creek they heard news of an attack on another survey party near Pine Bluffs, only a few miles over the border into Wyoming Territory. The attackers killed Lathrop Hills, one of their fellow surveyors, heightening their anxiety.[100] Finally, Ferguson's crew received carbines and ammunition for their protection.[101] While the westernmost crews were up Crow Creek in the Laramie Hills, Ferguson's survey crews laid out sidings and towns at Sidney, Antelope, and Dead Pine Bluffs. Another crew moved farther west to lay out a new town on Crow Creek, Cheyenne.

In July the rails passed through Sidney and at the end of August they were at Antelope (now called Kimball). It became widely known that Cheyenne would be the next winter headquarters and supply base. In short order the townspeople at Julesburg loaded their tents, supplies, and buildings on freight wagons and flat cars. For the most part they bypassed Sidney and headed for their next big opportunity in Cheyenne.

After only six months of an intense existence Julesburg Number Three was virtually abandoned. A few years later the railroad built a branch line to Denver, leaving the main line tracks three or four miles to the east. The population moved to the new junction, Julesburg Number Four, where it has been to this day and remains as the business center of the local area.

Photographer Eugene Arundel Miller.

**Fort Sidney Post Commander's House
preserved and restored.**

12. Sidney

*The Indians learned that the presence of survey
crews meant the iron rails would soon cut
through their traditional hunting grounds. Their
reaction was predictable – to fight back as best
they could.*

General Dodge picked a spot along the banks of
Crow Creek for the location of a major new railroad
town, Cheyenne. The new town would be the winter
base and a railroad supply center. It became a major
goal and had to be reached before the end of 1867.
However, the surveyors and construction crews were
still miles away and faced increasingly hostile Indians.

Up the Creek

The Indians watched warily from the surrounding ridges as the surveyors worked their way up Lodgepole Creek from Julesburg toward Crow Creek. As they set out a continuous line of stakes along the north side of Lodgepole Creek the Indians now understood what the stakes meant: they were being pushed farther and farther away from their traditional hunting grounds. The Indian raiders followed the survey crews westward and attacked them relentlessly. In one raid the raiders took the surveyors' pack mules and supplies but spared their lives. In another raid, Arthur Ferguson noted in his diary, a band of 800 Indians swarmed down the line and pulled up a mile of stakes within sight of the survey crew that had just set them out.[102] Not too long afterward a Cheyenne raiding party attacked another survey crew's camp and drove off 70 mules and horses.

Unfortunately, the survey crews had no rifles and were virtually unarmed. Soldiers, few as they were, protected the construction crews, leaving the surveyors to their own devices. The surveyors sent repeated pleas for help to the railroad officials and finally received a few rifles and ammunition. But still all did not go smoothly. One of Ferguson's crew was returning to camp after picking up a rifle and 500 rounds of ammunition, but he fell off a log while crossing Lodgepole Creek and all the ammunition went to the bottom of the creek, ruined.

In June the crew's anxiety heightened as they heard more about an Indian attack on the survey crew working near Crow Creek 100 miles farther west. The other crew chief, Lathrop Hill, had been reconnoitering far in advance of the rest of the crew when a group of

Cheyenne cut him off from his party, chased him about 15 miles, and savagely killed him. Ferguson's diary entry reflects his deep emotions over the killing.[103] A few weeks after the attack, Ferguson was sent to help recover Hill's body from where he had been buried in the open prairie, so that Hill could be reburied in a cemetery.

After repeated pleas for protection, a small contingent of soldiers arrived on Lodgepole Creek to establish Sidney Barracks. At about the same time the rails reached Sidney. Now with the protection of the soldiers, meager as it was, the town was designated as a railroad division point. assuring the town of some permanency.

The following year the Army enlarged the barracks facilities to house three companies of soldiers and added five officers' quarters, a guard house, hospital, laundry, bakery, and stables. The facilities also included storage warehouses for military supplies to support the other Army units in the region. A few years later the Barracks became Fort Sidney, but in the next twenty years the need for the Fort slowly faded and it was closed entirely. Most of the land and buildings were sold.

The Supply Problem
Starting early in 1867 the Casement brothers drove their construction crews hard. They were to reach Cheyenne before winter. Most railroad watchers were dubious, but during the summer the rail crews pushed well beyond Julesburg. In early August the graders and track layers hardly paused as they rolled on through the designated location for the new town of Sidney. To

reach Cheyenne before winter was now an achievable goal and efforts were redoubled to do just that.

For the railroad builders it was critically important to have sufficient materials close to the fast moving end of the line. In order to keep supplies close at hand Sidney became the railroad's fifth supply base. A steady stream of freight trains now rolled into the settlement where the rail cars were unloaded and all manner of material stockpiled, everything needed for the next one hundred miles of railroad.

As was often the case, ties were again in short supply. During the previous year as railroad construction crews passed through Nebraska timber became increasingly scarce. The railroad had a voracious appetite not only for ties (nearly 3,000 ties were needed for each mile) but thousands of telegraph poles were also needed, and boards for dozens of station buildings. The search for timber spread westward, well beyond the end of the rails. Early in 1867 the Casements contracted for 1,800 woodsmen and teamsters and sent them into the Black Hills (Laramie Mountains) and other Wyoming forests to search for suitable timber. There was good money to be made by the timber men and the response was tremendous. By the end of the season 100,000 ties were ready. Most had been hauled many miles from the forests to tie camps near the anticipated rail sidings. There, ties and poles were stacked, ready to haul to the end of the line.

Photograph by Arundel C. Hull.

The earliest known view of Sidney, Nebraska, 1868.
At the left is the new ten-stall roundhouse. Stacked ties stretch
along the siding behind the buildings. Flat cars loaded with
rock are in the foreground.

The appetite for all construction material was fierce.
Daily train loads moved westward from Omaha laden
with everything imaginable. The flow of supplies
improved greatly in January 1867 when a railroad was
completed across Iowa linking the East Coast suppliers
to Council Bluffs. Now freight need not be loaded on
steamers for the slow journey up the Missouri River but
could be ferried across the river directly to the Union
Pacific's eastern railhead in Omaha. For a few weeks in
the winter temporary tracks were even laid across the
river on the ice.

Getting a steady flow of rails, spikes, and other ironware
from the eastern suppliers became more manageable.
The challenge now was to accumulate a hefty supply of
those materials at the Sidney supply base so there
would be no hold up out on the line.

Sidney became important to the railroad for another reason. From Omaha to North Platte the rails climbed only six feet per mile, a relatively easy grade. Westward from North Platte the railroad climbed ten feet per mile. From Sidney westward, as the route approached mountain country, the surveyors found the grade would be steepened to about twenty feet per mile. It did not seem like much, not even noticeable to most observers, but it was important for future railroad operations. Because of the grade change, Sidney was selected as a railroad division point, a place to fill the water tanks, load up fuel, change crews, and repair equipment. As soon as the rail laying crews passed through the Sidney site, construction started on an impressive ten-stall brick roundhouse, turntable, and several other structures. The roundhouse was particularly welcomed by the station keepers and the few settlers in the vicinity because it also provided stockade type protection from the Indians. Within months a section house, freight house, and a water tank were also erected.

Into the 1870s the railroaders and settlers continued to be threatened by the periodic Indian raids. A treaty had forced tribes northward and cut them off from the great herds of buffalo, their traditional basis for survival. The government promised the tribes beef but the supply was woefully insufficient. Indian threats and reprisal raids frequently sent settlers and rail crews into the roundhouse where the brick walls and iron doors afforded great protection.[104]

Another Rough Town
Since there was still a lot of "street action" at Julesburg only a few of the gamblers and saloon keepers moved

into Sidney. New arrivals, however, were every bit as audacious as the ones who left. Sidney was not immune from the "hell-on-wheels" opportunists. There were just not so many of them. Tough woodsmen and teamsters added to the motley, highly antagonistic mix. Murders and deaths in drunken brawls were so common that they were scarcely noticed. Even the new weekly newspaper the *Sidney Telegraph* was blasé about the toughs who "died with their boots on."

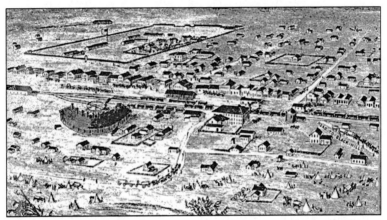

Nina Hull Miller Collection.
An artist's view of Sidney, Nebraska in 1879 portrays a town busy with both rail traffic and freight wagons.

When it became clear that the railroad's winter camp would be in Cheyenne it was good news for Sidney. Most of the toughs moved on and the Sidney "hell-on-wheels" town lasted only a few weeks.

When photographer Arundel Hull stepped down from a train in 1868 only a few railroad workers populated the place. As he looked about he saw precious little to photograph and almost no potential customers. He carried his bulky camera equipment and supplies up the hill north of the station for the one interesting view of the roundhouse and scattering of other buildings. After selling very few prints, he moved on to find better prospects.

Shoddy Work

Lodgepole Creek is fed by springs emerging from the hills many miles to the west. The water sometimes disappears in the sandy stream bottom and reappears miles downstream. Apparently, the streams looked deceiving to the masons who were building the bridge abutments and supports. At many of the crossings the "build-it-fast" crews simply carved the dirt back and stacked up facing stone on edge. The poor work often went undetected for months but after the spring rains in 1868, the inferior work became glaringly apparent. L. B. Boomer, the principal bridge contractor, whose crews were to set the prefabricated timber bridges in place, sent General Dodge a vehement protest. After a couple of experiences with his bridge work falling down Boomer refused to erect any more bridges on the "masonry" that had been erected by those particular contractors. He complained that the masonry is "failing to support their own weight, no cars having run over them." Dodge had seen some of the bad work along Lodgepole Creek and made a special trip out on the line to see for himself how widespread the problem was. He saw where three spans fell in as the abutments gave away and two arch culverts collapsed because the main support was only the facing stone. [105]

General Dodge lamented that, "We cannot trust the masons who have had the reputation of 'Being No. 1' unless we employ an engineer...to stand right over them!"

This drawing from *Leslie's Illustrated Newspaper* in 1877 reflects the freighting activity along the tracks at Sidney.

After the years of heavy construction supply train traffic, the rail activity at Sidney fell to one passenger train and one freight train each way each day. After a quiet period, however, Sidney again became busy. This time it became the major terminal for freight wagons headed north to Fort Robinson where 10,000 Indians were held on a reservation. Then gold was discovered in the Black Hills of South Dakota causing the rush of 1876-77. Sidney served as the closest rail connection and Sidney again became a bustling, brawling community. At the peak of activity there were reportedly 23 saloons along the main block. After a few more years, community outrage brought general lawlessness to a stop.

More Hazards

During the railroad construction years the presence of soldiers at Sidney Barracks seemed to do little to deter the audacious Indian attacks on the railroad and settlers. In April 1868 as a passenger train made a regular dinner stop at Sidney, the brakeman, C. C. Cope, stepped off the train and chatted with conductors Tom Cahoon and Wilkes Edmundson. They had ridden out planning to try a little fishing on nearby Lodgepole Creek. The three men spotted Indians along the bluffs overlooking the town but they decided they were friendly Pawnee. As the fishermen left for the Creek the train pulled away from the station and Cope slid open the baggage car door. He pulled up a trunk and sat down. With a loud *thwang* an arrow hit the side of the trunk right between Cope's legs. Fortunately, it was six inches low. "I didn't wait for a second arrow to come but closed the door and went to the locker where we kept about 15 Spencer rifles to use in case of attack, took out a Spencer, loaded it, pushed the door open just far enough to stick out the end of the rifle, and let go all the shot that was in it."

The two would-be fisherman, Cahoon and Edmundson, were not so fortunate. They were chased along the Creek and then cut off by the Indians who turned out to be Sioux not Pawnee. Cahoon was shot, severely wounded, and partially scalped. Edmundson, with several arrows in him, brandished his revolver and drove the Sioux away. Both men worked their way back along the Creek to the protection of town. Luckily, they survived their wounds. Cahoon worked many more years for the Union Pacific, but he wore his conductor's hat well back on his head to cover his scarred bald spot.

As a reaction to the increased Indian attacks, the soldiers and townspeople built a small stone fortification on the ridge just north of town. It was quite ineffective as a deterrent, and offered almost no protection. It was soon abandoned.

Fire was a hazard all along the railroad. Some fires were started by lightning strikes, some by the Indians, and some were started by surveyors to clear their line-of-sight when they were staking out the railroad location. When trains started traveling the rails, sparks from the locomotives frequently ignited the prairie grass. Usually grass fires burned themselves out. A fire on a train itself, however, was another matter.

On one occasion, a locomotive engineer, Robert Galbraith, loaded up with fuel in Sidney for a run to the west. The fuel was an unusual combination of cedar wood and soft Iowa coal. It produced plenty of sparks and lots of slag as it burned. As Galbraith set out, sparks blew back along the train and after a few miles the sparks set fire to two carloads of baled hay. The car just preceding the hay cars was loaded with mules. Wanting to protect the mules, Galbraith directed brakeman to cut the blazing hay cars loose, and as the cars rolled to a stop one of them fell over. With no recourse, Galbraith continued to the next station to telegraph others of the mishap and call for assistance.

Having now exhausted the locomotive's fuel supply, the fire dwindled and the locomotive lost steam. To restart boiler fire Galbraith first had to clear the slag from the firebox and find more fuel. Using a hammer and chisel he cut the slag from inside the firebox and tossed it onto the station platform. There the hot clinker promptly started the wooden platform afire. Galbraith and the brakeman frantically put out the platform fire but now had to find fuel for the locomotive. Using wood from the platform did not seem like a good idea so the two men cleverly pulled several ties out from under the track. They chopped them up, fed chunks into the boiler, restarted the fire, got up steam, and backed the train down the track to where they had left the burning hay cars.

The lead car on the train was now the car loaded with mules. The heat from the hay car fire apparently warped the tracks and the mule car derailed. As the mule car was cut loose it too overturned, freeing the terrified animals that ran off across the prairie. Galbraith and the brakemen gave up for the night, went back to the station, and found a place to sleep in bug infested grass. After a few unrecorded recovery events Galbraith was called back to North Platte. Because there was a shortage of locomotive engineers Galbraith neither lost his job nor was even reprimanded.[106]

As the track layers rolled on westward from Sidney they left in their wake the sidings and stations of Brownson, Potter, Dix, Antelope, Adams (now Oliver), and Bushnell. The first stations were old boxcars sitting on a side track. Local railroaders and settlers alike made good use of discarded ties and spilled coal. The village of Antelope was a coaling and telegraph station, with side tracks and a section house. The station and its clustered settlement were renamed in 1866 after Thomas Kimball, the railroad's General Manager.

Discarded wood ties are still sought after by many who live near the railroad.

Land and Cattle

Geographically, there is an imaginary north-south line just west of North Platte. Valuable farm land lies to the east and grazing land of lesser value to the west. The railroad was granted all odd-number sections, in a checkerboard pattern, for ten miles on both sides of the rails. The even-numbered sections remained government land open for sale or homesteading. Sales of the eastern farmland helped finance the railroad construction, but west of North Platte there were almost no land sales. The problem was the checkerboard system.

For grazing the ranchers needed large contiguous holdings. The cattleman could acquire railroad land cheaply but not the government land, because the price was fixed. As a result cattlemen simply chose not to buy any land. They ran their stock wherever they chose and paid nothing.

After fifteen years of free use of the open range the "big player" in the west, Bay State Livestock Co., bought about 250,000 acres of railroad land at $1 an acre. They continued as a "big player" in western Nebraska for years.

Photograph by Arundel C. Hull.

Pine Bluffs, just over the Nebraska border into Wyoming. The tie camp exemplified the bleakness that lay ahead.

13. New Challenges in Wyoming

Building through Nebraska the railroaders displayed the magnitude of their vision and dogged determination. They opened new lands to hundreds of eager settlers and homesteaders looking for their own opportunities.

Now that the rails had crossed Nebraska, follow-up crews continued the work: putting in rail sidings, digging wells, and building board stations, depots, and freight houses. Land agents in the east heavily advertized availability of land and the great opportunities that came with it. "Development of the West" had begun!

In Cheyenne, wintering crews built up stockpiles of construction supplies preparing for the grueling challenge of crossing Wyoming and beyond. They refined the pattern and pace that had developed across Nebraska. They now faced a new set of challenges, most notably the climb up "Sherman Hill," bridging Dale Creek, crossing the Great Divide desert, and searching for scarce water.

You can follow the railroaders in two companion volumes: *Railroad 1869 Along the Historic Union Pacific Across Wyoming* and *Railroad 1869 Along the Historic Union Pacific In Utah to Promontory.*

A TRAVELERS' GUIDE:
WHAT TO SEE - HOW TO FIND IT
IN NEBRASKA

A TRAVELERS' GUIDE:
WHAT TO SEE - HOW TO FIND IT
IN NEBRASKA

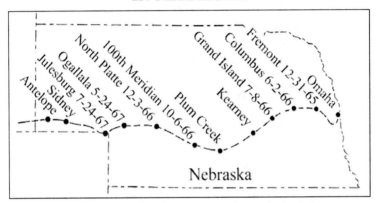

Union Pacific Construction Progress
Across Nebraska – 1864-1867.

Courtesy Union Pacific Railroad Museum.

"General Sherman" - Locomotive No. 1.

Omaha

In 1863 the investors in the newly organized Union Pacific Railroad maneuvered for their personal positions and set the stage for the monumental construction effort. Once President Lincoln approved the location of the future river crossing there was great celebration, but actual work faltered. After a year the railroad had completed only forty six miles of track. It would take two more years to cross Nebraska, then two more to join up with the Central Pacific at Promontory, Utah.

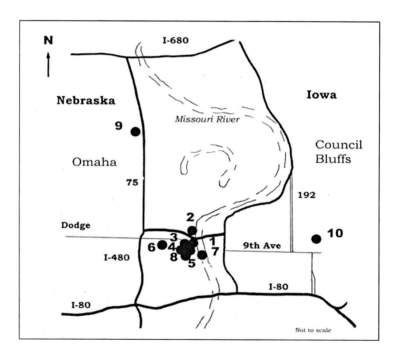

Vicinity Map - Omaha and Council Bluffs.

Omaha

1. The Ground Breaking. The site is at the foot of Davenport Street at 10th Street, under the present day I-480 overpass. (Sorry, little of historical interest remains.)

2. Start of Grading and Ferry Landing. The grading apparently started near the foot of Chicago Street at 7th Street, along present day Abbot Drive. The Great Excursionists disembarked at a ferry landing in about this same location. The area has been developed into the attractive Lewis and Clark Landing Riverfront Park.

3. Herndon House (International Hotel). The hotel was at the northeast corner of Farnam and 9th Streets. The location is occupied by a parking structure that also occupies an abandoned section of 9th Street.

4. Old Market Area. This historic area is between 10th and 13th Street and Jackson and Harney. There is an array of preserved buildings with shops and restaurants.

5. Central Block and Ware Block. These buildings faced each other across Farnam Street at 13th Street. The site of the Ware Block has become a beautiful urban park.

6. Hull's Panorama of Omaha

Hull's early photograph was taken from Farnam at about 18th Street. A present day view toward the east reveals the only recognizable feature from 1868 to be the river in the distance.

Photograph by Arundel C. Hull.

7. Missouri River Bridge. For a view of the river front go east on one-way Douglas, turn left on 8th Street, then right to one of the parking areas at the Lewis and Clark Landing Riverside Park.

8. Durham Western History Museum

801 South 10th Street, Omaha, Nebraska 68108
402-444-5071 www.dwhm.org.

The museum, a "must see," is in the old Union Station. In addition to the magnificently restored waiting room the museum include photograph galleries, and train cars at the track level.

9. General Crook House Museum
Douglas County Historical Society
Fort Omaha (30th and Fort)
5730 North 30th Street
Omaha, Nebraska 86111
402-455-9990 www.omahshistory.org
From the Old Market area of Omaha, get on I-480 westbound, then I-440 (same as State 75) northbound about 8 miles. Exit on 30th Avenue North, and then continue on 30th Street about 3 blocks, then left on Jaynes Street into Fort Omaha. Follow the signs.

10. Union Pacific Railroad Museum
200 Pearl Street
Council Bluffs, Iowa 51503
712-329-8307
From Omaha, go east on I-80, then cross the Missouri River Bridge, to Exit 3 in Council Bluffs, Iowa. Go north on 192 Expressway. (192 then continues as South 6th Street.) Turn right on Willow, 1 block, then right again on Pearl Street.

This premier museum is the center of Union Pacific Railroad historical records.

Elkhorn and Fremont

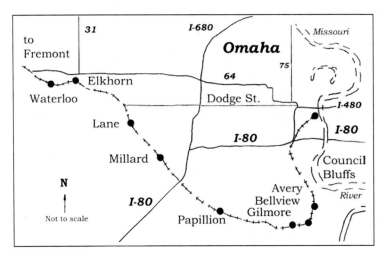

The Oxbow Route

1. The Oxbow Route from Omaha to Elkhorn

There are still rails along most of the route but also a profusion of other tracks. For the adventuresome:

Go south out of central Omaha on 24th Street. At "W" Street, 24th Street changes into Railroad Avenue. Continue on Railroad Ave. The railroad is on the west side of the freeway for about a half mile, then crosses under the freeway and is adjacent to Railroad Avenue. Railroad Avenue merges into Fort Crook Road. Continue on Fort Crook Road.

At Cornhusker Road turn west toward Papillion. Here there are no public roads beside the railroad. The route has been abandoned and the rails pulled up.

Past Papillion turn north on 108th Street, then west on Harrison Street under I-80 onto Harry Anderson Drive.

Follow Harry Anderson Drive west. The road is directly next to the old railroad. As you approach Millard, the rails are still in place and in service. At Millard merge onto 132nd Street. Continue to intersection of US-275 and NE-50.

Continue on US-275 (Industrial Road) west from Millard. West of Millard 2.5 miles US-275 curves westerly and becomes West Center Road. Four miles west, turn right (north) on 204th Street. Continue north 3 miles to the railroad crossing and West Papillion Creek at Elkhorn.

2. Elkhorn A small but pretty town. Regretfully, no features of railroad history remain at Elkhorn. Just south of the railroad over-crossing, turn east toward the library to Park Road. Turn left on Park Road to Main Street. Turn right on Main Street; cross Papillion Creek and Railroad, or continue on Cedar west to Athletic Field Park.

Fremont

From Elkhorn proceed northwest about 18 miles to US-30 at Fremont (23rd Street). Go west about a mile to Nye Street then south 6 blocks to the May Museum.

1. Louise E. May Museum
Dodge County Historical Society
1643 North Nye Avenue
Fremont, Nebraska 68025
402-721-4515 www.maymuseum@juno.com

Arundel C. Hull, the young photographer who took many of the photographs presented in **Railroad 1869**, opened a studio in Fremont, married, and spent the rest of his life as one of the town's notable citizens. The Hull family members were friends of the Nye family whose mansion has been preserved as the May Museum. The mansion was built in 1874 for the town's first mayor. The richly finished oak and mahogany interior holds memorable collections of the Dodge County Historical Society, as well as exhibits and recreated rooms of the 19th and early 20th century.

2. Fremont and Elkhorn Valley Railroad
(An excursion train.)
1835 North Somers Ave.
Fremont, Nebraska 68025
402-727-0615 www.fremontrailroad.com

Columbus

1. Loup River RR Bridge
A modern steel bridge now occupies the site of the original 1867 wood trestle.

Entering Columbus from the east, follow US-30 to the center of town, 33rd Ave. Turn left (south) on 33rd Ave. (also US-30), one mile, cross the UP railroad tracks, then go one block to 8th Street.
Turn right (west) on 8th Street, travel ½ mile to Lottie Lane.
Turn left (south) on Lottie Lane, 0.6 mile as Lottie Lane curves to the right, to Deer River Road.
Turn left (south), then follow the curving Deer River Road 0.9 mile to the gravel parking area at the end.

2. Platte County Historical Society Museum
2916 16th Street
Columbus, Nebraska 68601
402-564-4553   402-564-6436
Among numerous historic displays, the museum features the 1857 cabin of one of the town founders, Frederick Gottschalk, with many of the cabin's original furnishings.

Grand Island

1. Stuhr Museum of the Prairie Pioneer
3133 West Highway 34 (at US 281)
P.O. Box 1505
Grand Island, Nebraska 86601
308-385-5316 www.stuhrmuseum.org
From I-80 take Exit 312, north on US 34, 4
miles.
Then turn right (east) on Husker Highway (US
34) 0.2 miles to entrance.

This outstanding museum includes numerous
Nebraska history exhibits both inside the
dramatic Stuhr Building and over the 200 acre
complex, including a 1890s railroad town.

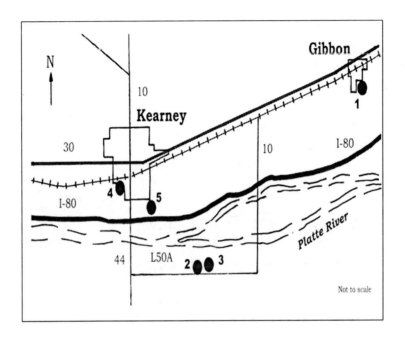

Vicinity Map - Gibbon and Kearney

Kearney

1. Gibbon Heritage Center
(In a former church.)
2nd and Court Street
P. O. Box 116
Gibbon, Nebraska 68840
308-468-5509
I-80 Exit 285. Go north 3 miles.
2nd Street is two blocks before the railroad crossing.

2. Dobytown Historical Marker
I-80 Exit 272. Go south on Highway 44, 2 miles to 50A, then east (left) on 50A, 4 miles.

3. Fort Kearny State Historical Park
1020 V Road
Kearney, Nebraska 68847
I-80 Exit 272. Go south on Highway 44, 1+ miles to L50A, then east (left) on L50A, 4 miles.

4. Rails and Trails Museum
710 West 11th Street (Box 523)
Kearney, Nebraska 68845
308-234-3041
I-80 Exit 272. Go north on 2nd Avenue 1 mile to 11th Street, then west (left) on 11th Street 0.2 mile.

(Cont.) The Rails and Trails Museum is housed in an old depot building. Exhibits include transportation, a log cabin, and other early buildings.

5. Great Platte River Archway Monument
3060 East 1st Street
Kearney, Nebraska 68845
308-237-1000   877-511-2724
I-80 Exit 272. Go north on 2nd Avenue 0.2 mile to Talmadge Road.
Go east on Talmadge Road 0.2 miles to Central Avenue, then south on Central Avenue 0.2 mile to East 1st Street (Archway Parkway).
Go east 0.8 mile on East 1st Street (Archway Parkway).

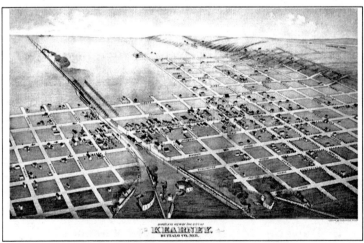

Artist's View of Kearney - 1870s.

Plum Creek (Lexington)

1. Plum Creek Massacre Marker

I-80 Exit 237. Go south on Highway 283 and cross the Platte River Bridge.

One half mile past the bridge Highway 283 curves to the right (west.) At the end of the curve turn left (south) onto the county road, proceed 2 miles. Turn left (east) on the county road, ½ mile. Turn right (south) on the county road, 1 mile. Turn left (east) on the county road, 5 miles. Turn right (south) on the county road, 1 mile. Turn left (east) on County Road 748, proceed about 4 miles. The marker is on the left (north) side of the road.

2. Original Plum Creek Station Site, and Freeman's Store site

I-80 Exit 237. Proceed north 2 miles, over the railroad to 6th Street. Turn right (east) on 6th Street about 5 blocks to Taft Street, then turn right (south) on Taft Street, to its intersection with Highway 30.

The original depot site is east of Taft Street, unmarked, among the industrial facilities. Freeman's store site is east of Taft Street unmarked and likely just north of Highway 30.

3. Dawson County Historical Museum

805 North Taft Street
Lexington, Nebraska 68850
308-324-5340

(Cont.) I-80 Exit 237. Proceed north about 2 miles, over the railroad and continue 3 blocks to East 6th Street. Turn right (east) on East 6th Street, 5 blocks to Taft Street. Turn left (north) on Taft Street 1½ blocks to the museum entrance on the left (west).

Nina Hull Miller Collection.

A temporary side track carries rail traffic around the 1867 derailment.

4. Plum Creek Train Derailment Monument
From I-80 Exit 237 proceed north 2 miles, and cross over the railroad. At next intersection turn right and double back to westbound US Highway 30. Go west on Highway 30 about 2 miles. The monument is on the south side of the highway.

Grand Excursion (Cozad)

1. 100ᵗʰ Meridian Museum
206 East 8ᵗʰ Street (P. O. Box 325)
Cozad, Nebraska 69130
308-784-1100
From I-80 Exit 222 proceed north one mile on
Highway 21 (also called Meridian Avenue).
Cross the railroad to 8ᵗʰ Street. Turn left (west)
on 8ᵗʰ Street. The museum is on the right (north)
side of the street.

2. Depot Museum
Highway 30 at Meridian Avenue
Cozad, Nebraska 69130
For open times check at the 100ᵗʰ Meridian
Museum 308-784-1100.

The Union Pacific depot originally faced the
railroad. It was turned around to face Highway
30 when it was acquired for use as a museum.

3. The 100ᵗʰ Meridian (actual)
From the center of town proceed west on
Highway 30. About a quarter mile past Avenue O
the highway crosses the actual 100ᵗʰ Meridian;
however, this location is unmarked.

4. Camp No 2. site (Platte City)
On I-80 or on Highway 30 proceed west from
Cozad about 27 miles past Brady to Maxwell (I-
80 Exit 190). The site is now covered with trees
and is unmarked.

5. Fort McPherson National Cemetery
12004 South Spur 56A
Maxwell, Nebraska 69151
308-582-4433 888-737-2800
From I-80 Exit 190 proceed south on State
Highway 56A 2 miles. Fort McPherson is on the
right (west).

6. Gothenburg
Although the town was founded nearly two
decades after the railroad was built it is
historically interesting.

7. Pony Express Station in Ehmen Park
514 15th Street
Gothenburg, Nebraska 69138
308-537-3505 800-482-5520
Highway I-80 Exit 211, north on Lake Avenue to
15th Street.
The station was originally on the Oregon Trail.
Used by the Pony Express 1860-61. The station
was reconstructed in 1931.

8. Sod House Museum
300 South Lake Ave.
Gothenburg, Nebraska 69138
Chamber of Commerce 308-537-5505
Highway I-80 Exit 211 one block north.

North Platte

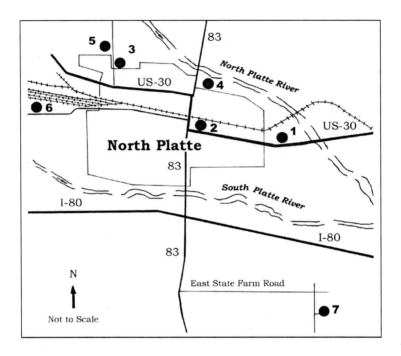

Vicinity Map - North Platte

North Platte

1. Railroad Bridge over the North Platte River

I-80 Exit 177, north on Dewey Street (one way) 1¼ miles, and converge onto Jeffers Street.

Continue north on Jeffers Street, cross the overpass, 4 blocks to the Rodeo Road (12th Street) intersection at Highway US 30.

Turn east (right) on Highway US 30.

At 2 miles, view the railroad bridge on the left as you round the curve and approach the railroad over crossing. (Sorry, no public access to the bridge itself.)

2. Depot Site and Historical Marker
(WWII North Platte Canteen)

I-80 Exit 177, then north on Dewey Street (one way) 1¼ miles and converge onto Jeffers Street.

Continue north on Jeffers Street to 4th Street.

Turn east (right) on 4th Street, 3 blocks to Chestnut Street.

Turn north (left) on Chestnut, 3 blocks to Front Street.

In the early 1900s the original wood frame depot building was replaced with a new masonry building. During World War II the depot then served as a "canteen" for more than six million servicemen traveling cross country by rail. It has now been removed to leave a small park with a commemorative monument.

3. Lincoln County Historical Museum
2403 North Buffalo Bill Avenue
North Platte, Nebraska 69101-9702
308-534-5640 800-955-4528
I-80 Exit 177, then north on Dewey Street (one way) 1¼ miles, and converge onto Jeffers Street. North on Jeffers Street. Cross the overpass, and go 4 blocks to Rodeo Drive (12th Street).
Turn west (left) on Rodeo Drive (US 30) 1½ miles to North Buffalo Bill Avenue. Turn north (right) on North Buffalo Bill Avenue 0.5 mile.
The museum is on the right.

4. Cody Park Railroad Museum
(and Locomotive Display)
1400 North Jeffers Street
North Platte, Nebraska, 69101
308-532-6770
I-80 Exit 177, then north on Dewey Street (one way) 1¼ miles and converge onto Jeffers Street. North on Jeffers Street, cross the overpass to 16th Street. Cody Park is on the right.

The railroad display includes a "Challenger" type locomotive, various rail cars, and other railroad memorabilia.

5. Buffalo Bill State Historical Park
North Buffalo Bill Avenue (P. O. Box 229)
North Platte, Nebraska 69101-9706
308-535-8035 800-826-7276
I-80 Exit 177, then north on Dewey Street (one way) 1¼ miles and converge onto Jeffers Street. Continue north on Jeffers Street (it becomes US 30), cross the overpass to Rodeo Drive (12th Street).

Turn west (left) on Rodeo Drive, (US 30) 1½ miles to North Buffalo Bill Avenue.
Turn north (right) on Buffalo Bill Avenue 1 mile. The park is on the left.

The park is the former Scout's Rest Ranch, with original mansion and other buildings, interpretive displays, and exhibits.

6. Golden Spike Tower and Visitor Center
1249 North Homestead Road
North Platte, Nebraska 69101
308-532-9920

Open Seasonally. Call for times.

I-80 Exit 177, then north on Dewey Street (one way) 1¼ miles and converge onto Jeffers Street. Continue north on Jeffers Street, an additional 2 blocks to 4th Street. Turn west (left) on 4th Street, one block.

(Cont.) Turn north (right) on Vine Street, then 3 blocks to Front Street.

Turn west (left) on Front Street 4¼ miles, then around the curve to right, ¼ mile to the **Golden Spike Tower and Visitor Center.**

The Tower affords a panoramic view of Union Pacific's Bailey Yard, the world's largest railroad classification yard. It covers 2,850 acres and stretches for eight miles, west of North Platte.

Every 24 hours the Bailey Yard handles 10,000 rail cars. Cars are sorted in "hump yards" then four cars a minutes are gently rolled along any of 114 "bowl" tracks to make up trains headed for dozens of destinations.

At the Tower the viewing floors are accessible by elevator or stairs. On the enclosed 8th floor, there is a 360 degree view of the entire valley. The 7th floor is open, allowing viewers to both watch and hear the action going on below.

7. Oregon Trail Marker and Jack Morrow Ranch

I-80 Exit 177. South on State Highway 83, 1½ miles, then east on East State Farm Road 2.6 miles. South on Hidden Lakes Road (Old Highway 83 Road) 0.4 mile. The monument is at the driveway to private property.

Ogallala

1. Old Town Front Street Crystal Palace (replica)
519 East First Street (Highway 30)
Ogallala, Nebraska 69153
308-284-9988 (Mercantile store.)
I-80 Exit 126, then north on Highway 61/26 over the river and over the railroad.
Turn right (east) 3 blocks. Turn right again (south) to return to 1st Street.

2. Mansion on the Hill (and museum) (restored 1880s brick mansion)
West 10th and Spruce Street
Ogallala, Nebraska 69153
308-284-4327
From I-80 Exit 126 turn north on Highway 61/26 over the river and over the railroad.
Continue north to East 8th Street, then turn left (west) 1 block to Spruce.
Turn right (north) 2 blocks to 10th Street. The mansion is on the corner.

3. Boot Hill Cemetery
10th Street at Parkhill Drive
From I-80 Exit 126 turn north on Highway 61/26 over the river and over the railroad.
Continue north to East 8th Street. Turn left (west) 1 block to Spruce. Then turn right (north) 2 blocks to 10th Street. Turn left (west) five blocks.
Turn right (north) on Parkhill Drive.
This picturesque early cemetery is on the left.

Julesburg

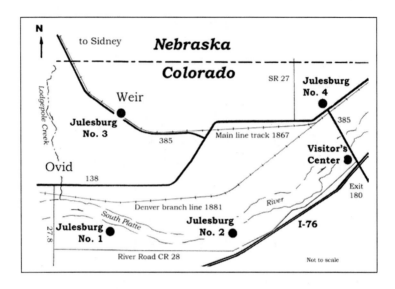

Map showing Four Julesburgs

1. Fort Sedgwick Museum
114 East 1st Street
Julesburg, Colorado 80737
970-474-2061 www.kci.net/history
I-76 Exit 180, then north on Highway 385, 1 mile, cross the railroad tracks into downtown. Turn right (east) on East First Street, one block. The museum is on the left.

2. Julesburg Depot Museum (Julesburg No. 4)
201West 1st Street
Julesburg, Colorado 80737
970-474-2264

(Cont.) From I-76 Exit 180 proceed north on Highway 385, 1 mile, cross the railroad tracks into downtown.
Turn left (west) on East First Street, 1-1/2 blocks. The Depot Museum is on the left.

3. Julesburg No. 2
Go west on Country Road 28, 2.8 miles to the marker. The site is private property north of the road. No buildings remain.
The site is just outside the four-mile boundary of Fort Sedgwick Military Reservation where liquor sales were prohibited.

4. Jules Beni Stage Station and Julesburg No. 1
Continue west on County Road 28, 3.5 miles to the marker.
The town was burned by Indians in 1865 and was abandoned.
The site is private property north of the road.

5. Fort Sedgwick (site)
Continue west on County Road 28, 0.9 mile to the marker. A flag pole marking the site is north of the road. After being closed in 1871, most buildings were dismantled and shipped to Sidney Barracks.
The site is now private property.

6. Julesburg No. 3
From downtown Julesburg (No. 4) go west on 138 3.5 miles, then right on 385. Go 2 miles to Weir (Julesburg No. 3).

Sidney

1. Lodgepole Depot Museum
Lodgepole, Nebraska
Open by appointment. For hours call Cheyenne County Visitors Committee at the Chamber of Commerce in Sidney, 800-421-4769.
I-80 Exit 76, then proceed north on Road 149, 2.6 miles. Before the railroad turn left on Front Street.

2. Fort Sidney Museum and Post Commander's House
1108 6th Avenue (at Jackson)
Sidney, Nebraska 69162
308-254-2150

From I-80 Exit 59, proceed north on Highway 17J, 2 miles to Highway 30.
Turn left (west) on Highway 30, (becomes Illinois Street), 1.4 miles to 6th Avenue, then left (south) on 6th Avenue one block.

The historic district is now a residential area. It includes the Commander's House built in 1871, officers' duplex quarters built in 1884, and the powder magazine. The Post Commander's House and the Officers' Duplex have been restored and are used as a museum.

3. Fort Sidney Powder House
1045 5th Avenue
Sidney, Nebraska 69162

**Fort Sidney Museum
and Post Commander's House.**

Potter and Antelope (Kimball)

1. Potter Depot Museum. Open by appointment. For hours call Cheyenne County Visitors Committee at the Chamber of Commerce in Sidney, Nebraska
308-254-5851 800-421-4769.
From I-80 Exit 38, go north on SR 17B Link (becomes Chestnut Street) 0.7 mile, cross Highway 30 and the railroad tracks to Front Street.

2. Antelope (Kimball)
Plains Historical Museum
2nd and Chestnut Street
Kimball, Nebraska 69145
Open irregularly. Call to confirm times.
308-235-3889.
From I-80 take Exit 20, then proceed north on SR 71 (it becomes South Chestnut Street) 1.3 miles. Cross Highway 30 (3rd Street), and continue 2 blocks into downtown.
The museum is on the west side of the street.

Acknowledgements and Photo Credits

A very special thanks goes to David H. Bain, Lecturer, English Department at Middlebury College, Vermont and author of *"Empire Express,"* for stimulating my interest and solidifying my resolve to add Arundel Hull's photographs and travel experiences to the magnificent story of the first transcontinental railroad. I also have many other people to thank for their assistance. The following have been especially generous with their time.

John Bromley, Director Historic Projects, Union Pacific Railroad Museum, Council Bluffs, Iowa.

Jim Kroll, Manager, Myron Vallier, and others, Denver Public Library, Western History.

Patty Manhart, Director, Louise E. May Museum, Fremont, Nebraska.

Clare Mares, Eastern Nebraska Genealogical Society, Fremont, Nebraska.

Barry Swackhamer, historian and author, San Jose, California.

Mary McKinstry and Julie Thomas, Fort Sedgwick Historical Society Museum at Julesburg, Colorado.

Robert Manasek, Curator, Scotts Bluff National Monument, Gering, Nebraska.

Chad Wall and Mary Jo Miller, Nebraska State Historical Society, Lincoln, Nebraska.

Lou Schmitz, Omaha, Nebraska, for use of a map of the Oxbow Route.

Railroad 1869 through Nebraska

Betty Tremain, Terry Christopher, Judge Thomas Dorwart, Cheyenne County Historical Association, Sidney, Nebraska.

Francis and Ruth Fagot and Don Magnuson, Dawson County Historical Museum, Lexington, Nebraska.

Gregory P. Ames, Curator, The Saint Louis Mercantile Library, Saint Louis, Missouri.

Carl Mautz, publisher, Nevada City, California.

John Signor, author, editor, *Streamliner Magazine*, Dunsmuir, California.

Bob Spude, National Park Service Historian, Santa Fe, New Mexico.

United States Geological Survey, Photographic Archive, Denver, Colorado.

Photo Credits

All photographs by Arundel C. Hull and all unattributed photographs are from the author's collections. My thanks to the following organizations which have generously provided various photographs/illustrations and granted permission to publish them.

Colorado State Historical Society

Denver Public Library, Western History Department

Nebraska State Historical Society

National Park Service, Scotts Bluff National Monument

National Park Service, Golden Spike Nat'l Historic Site

Saint Louis Mercantile Library, Saint Louis, Missouri

Union Pacific Railroad Museum

United States Geological Survey Earth Science Photographic Archives

Utah State Historical Society

Wyoming State Archive

Bibliography

Ambrose, Stephen E., *Nothing Like it in the World, the Men Who Built the Transcontinental Railroad, 1863-1869,* New York, Simon and Schuster, 2000.

Andreas, *Andreas' History of the State of Nebraska,* Chicago, Western Historical Company, www.kancoll.org/books/andreas-ne_1882.

Bain, David Haward, *Empire Express, Building the First Transcontinental Railroad,* New York, Penguin Putman, 1999.

Bain, David Haward, *The Old Iron Road, An Epic of Rails, Roads, and the Urge to go West,* New York, Penguin Group, 2004.

Bartels, James M. and James J. Reisdorff, *Historical Railroads of Nebraska,* Charleston, Arcadia Publishing 2002.

Best, Gerald M., *Iron Horses to Promontory,* San Marino, Golden West Books, 1969.

Bratt, John, *Trails of Yesteryear,* Lincoln, University of Nebraska Press,1921 and 1949.

Brey, William, *Carbutt and the Union Pacific's Grand Excursion to the 100th Meridian,* SteroWorld, May-June,1980. http://CPRR.org/Museum/Stereo_World/Carbutt.

Buffalo Tales, Buffalo County Historical Society, V1, N5, May 1978; V4, N2, Feb. 1981; V6, N2, Feb. 1983; V10, N8, Sept. 1987; V11, N6, June 1988; V14, N3, March 1991; V23, N1, Jan.-Feb. 2000; V23, M2, Mar.-Apr. 2000, Kearney, Nebraska.

Butler, Anne M., *Daughters of Joy, Sisters of Misery, Prostitutes in the American West 1865-90,* Urbana and Chicago, University of Illinois Press, 1985.

Combs, Barry B., *The Bellevue Scare.*

Combs, Barry. *Westward to Promontory, Building the Union Pacific Across the Plains and Mountains,* Palo Alto, American West Publishing Company.

Czaplewski, Russ, *Plum Creek to Lexington 1866-1939,* Kearney Dawson County Historical Society, Morris Publishing, 1989.

Dunn, Ruth, *Attack on Black Kettle's Village and the Prelude to Sand Creek,* North Platte, 1973.

Dunn, Ruth, *Indian Vengeance at Julesburg,* North Platte, 1972.

Dunn, Ruth, *The Burning of Julesburg,* North Platte, 1973.

Eckberg, Scott B. *The Frontier Index: Chronicle of a World on Wheels,* ParkNet, National Park Service, 1981. http://nps.govp/research/world_on_wheels.htm.

Ehernberger, James L., *Grand Island Time Line, Grand Island After the War,* Streamliner, V16, N2, Cheyenne, Union Pacific Historical Society, 2002,

Ferguson, Arthur N., *Diary of Judge A. N Ferguson, Campaign of 1865, Surveys of the Union Pacific Railroad; Part II Campaign of 1866; Part III, Campaign of 1867, 5th Corps Journal, Corps of Engineers on Construction U. P. R. R.* Nebraska State Historical Society, Lincoln, Nebraska.

Ferguson, Arthur N., *Transcription of the Personal Diary, January 1868 – May 1869,* Utah History Research Center, Salt Lake City, Utah.

Fort Sedgwick Historical Society, *The History of Sedgwick County* Colorado, Dallas, National Share Graphics, 1982.

Freeman, Leigh, *Frontier Index, Julesburg, July 26, 1867, Fort Sanders, Wyoming, May 6, 1868, Green River, Wyoming, August 11, 1868, Bear River City, Oct. 30, 1868.*

Grinnell, George Bird, *Two Great Scouts and Their Pawnee Battalion,* reprinted from the original 1928 edition, Lincoln, Nebraska, University of Nebraska Press, 1973.

Hamaker, Gene E., *Locating Kearney Junction*, Buffalo Tales, Kearney, Nebraska, Buffalo County Historical Society, February 1981, V4, N4.

History, The, of Sedgwick, County Colorado, Fort Sedgwick Historical Society, Dallas, Texas, National ShareGraphics Inc. 1982.

Howell, Alice Shaneyfelt, *Early Days in Elm Creek*, Buffalo Tales, Kearney, Nebraska, Buffalo County Historical Society, February 1983, V6, N1.

Johnson, Mrs. Roy, et al, *Elkhorn Nebraska, 1867-1967, The First Century of Progress*, Elkhorn Nebraska, Elkhorn Woman's Club, 1967.

Keith County Historical Society, *How the West Was Lost, A History of Ogallala and Keith County*, Ogallala, Goodall City Library.

Kimball, Beverly Murray, *Ft. Kearney, Guardian of the Plains*, Kearney, Nebraska, Buffalo Tails, Buffalo County Historical Society, June 1988, V11, N6.

Klein, Maury, *Union Pacific, The Birth of a Railroad 1862-1893*, Garden City, New York, Doubleday and Company Inc., 1987.

Klein, Maury, *The Overland Route: First Impression*, Streamliner, Union Pacific Historical Society, Cheyenne, Wyoming, April 1988, V4, N2, Pp 16-21.

Kratville, William, *Railroads of Omaha and Council Bluffs*, Charleston South Carolina, Arcadia Publishing, 2002.

Laramie Plains Museum, Laramie, Wyoming.

Lee, Wayne C., *Wild Towns of Nebraska*, Caldwell, Idaho, Goodall City Library, Caxton Printing, 1988.

Lent, John A., *The Press On Wheels, A History of the Frontier Index of Nebraska, Colorado, Wyoming and Elsewhere?* Annals of Wyoming, 43:2:310.

Miller, Eugene A., *Photographer of the Early West, the Story of Arundel Hull*, Mill Valley, California, Antelope-Press, 2004.

Miller, Nina Hull, *Shutters West*, Denver, Sage Books, 1962.

Moulton, Candy, *Roadside History of Nebraska,* Missoula, Montana, Mountain Press Publishing Company, 1997.

Railroad 1869 through Nebraska

Nielsen, Elaine, *Ogallala, A Century on the Trail*, Ogallala, Keith County Historical Society, 1984.

O'Dell, Roy Paul and Kenneth C. Jessen, *An Ear In His Pocket, The Life of Jack Slade*, Loveland, Colorado, J. V. Publications, 1996.

O'Brian, Rhonda, *Margaret Trunks and John Reddy, Pioneer Railroaders and Farmers*, Kearney, Nebraska, Buffalo County Historical Society, V14, N3 1991.

Omaha World Herald, *Plum Creek Massacre 100 Years Ago Today*, Omaha, Nebraska, August 7, 1964.

Schmitz, Lou, *The Construction Years*, Streamliner, Cheyenne, Wyoming, Union Pacific Historical Society, A-M-J 1989, V5, N2, P 3-12.

Schmitz, Lou, *Union Pacific Railroad, Chronology of Omaha - Council Bluffs Events, The First 50 Years, 1862-1912*, (Unpublished) 2006.

Scott, Bob, *Slade, the True Story of the Notorious Badman*, Glendo, Wyoming, High Plains Press, 2004.

Scoville, C. H., *History of the Elkhorn Valley Nebraska*. Chicago/Omaha, National Publishing Company, 1892.

Seymour, Silas, *Incidents of a Trip Through the Great Platte Valley to the Rocky Mountains and Laramie Plains, in the Fall of 1866*, New York, D. Von Nostrand, 1867.

Shearer, Fredrick E., *The Pacific Tourist, Adams and Bishops Illustrated Transcontinental Guide of Travel from the Atlantic to the Pacific Ocean*, New York, Bounty Books, Division of Crown Publishers Inc., 1884.

Signor, John R., *Council Bluffs, A Union Pacific Town*, Streamliner, Union Pacific Historical Society, Cheyenne Wyoming, Spring 2006, V20, N2, P 7-32.

Signor, John R., Don Strack, James Ehernberger, and Andy Kirol, *The Aspen and Altamont Tunnels*, Streamliner, Union Pacific Historical Society, Cheyenne Wyoming, Fall 2005, V19, N4, P 7-32.

Stansbery, Karyn, *Boot Hill, Tombstone History of Ogallala*, Ogallala, Nebraska, Keith County News, Sept 18, 1996, p 6.

Steele, Volney, M.D., *Survivors of Scalping: The Frontier,* Journal of the West V44, N1, Santa Barbara, ABC-CLIO, 2005.

Stone, Irving, *Men to Match My Mountains, The Opening of the Far West 1840-1900,* Garden City, New York, Doubleday and Company, 1956.

Swackhamer, Barry A. Personal collection, Microfilm, *Frontier Index – July 26, 1867 – Nov 17, 1868,* Bancroft Library, University of California Berkeley.

Thompson, Anthony W. and Robert J. Church, *Railroad History in Photographs, 150 Years of American Railroading.,* Westford, Massachusetts, Signature Press in Association with the Railway and Locomotive Historical Society, 1996.

Vifquain, Sally, *Fort Kearny, The Rest of the Story, Part I,* Kearney, Buffalo County Historical Society, V23, N1, 2000.

Vifquain, Sally, *Fort Kearny, The Rest of the Story, Part II,* Kearney, Buffalo County Historical Society, V23, N2, 2000.

White, Tom, *On Unsettled Plains,* Nebraskaland, V80, N8, Lincoln, Nebraska Game and Parks Commission, 2002.

Williams, Dallas, *Hell Hole on the Platte,* Julesburg, Colorado, Fort Sedgwick Historical Society, 1996.

Williams, John Hoyt, *A Great and Shining Road, The Epic Story of the Transcontinental Railroad,* Lincoln, University of Nebraska Press, 1988.

Wilson, D. Ray, *Fort Kearny on the Platte,* Dundee, Illinois, Crossroads Communications, 1980.

Wilson, D. Ray, *Nebraska Historical Tour Guide, 2nd Edition,* Carpenterville, Illinois, Crossroads Communications, 1988.

Wisroth, Ethel M., *Texas Trail, Kimball Country Nebraska, 100 Years, 1888-1988,* Dallas, Texas, Curtis Media Corporation, 1988.

Wolff, A. J. "Jack", *Sidney Nebraska, The Way it Was,* Streamliner, V19, N4, Cheyenne, Union Pacific Historical Society, 2005.

End Notes

1 Schmitz, The Construction Years, 4.

2 Bain, 225.

3 Bain, 242.

4 Schmitz, The Construction Years, 6.

5 Klein, 74.

6 Schmitz, The Construction Years, 4.

7 Seymour ,52.

8 Ibid.

9 Schmitz, Chronology (Unpublished).

10 Schmitz, The Construction Years, 11.

11 Signor, 7.

12 Ibid.

13 Ferguson, diary July 1865.

14 Ferguson, diary August 3, 1865.

15 Andreas, Elkhorn Station.

16 Johnson et al.

17 Andreas, Elkhorn Station.

18 Shearer, 23.

19 Bain, 261.

20 Ambrose, 268.

21 Ferguson diary August 5,1865.

22 Ferguson diary August 13,1865.

23 Ambrose, 176.

24 Ibid.

25 Wilson, Tour Guide, 55.

26 Bain, 268.

27 Ferguson diary, August 14, 1865.

28 Ferguson diary, August 15,1866.

29 Bain, 265.

30 Bain, 267.

31 Ibid.

32 Bain, 268.

33 Klein, 98.

34 Bain, 328.

35 Ferguson diary, April 25, 1867.

36 Ferguson diary, July 28, 1866.

37 Ibid, August 7, 1866.

38 Ibid, August 18, 1866.

39 Ibid, August 21, 1866.

40 O'Brien, 3.

41 Vifquain, Part I, 1.

42 Kimball, 3.

43 Wilson, 173.

44 Ferguson diary, August 21, 1866.

45 Hamaker, 3.

46 Bain, 286.

47 Howell, 2.

48 Ibid.

49 Lent, 166.

50 Ferguson diary, September 9, 1866.

51 Omaha World Herald, August 7, 1964.

52 Shearer, 35.

53 Bain, 387-389.

54 Steele, 73.

55 Shearer, 36.

56 Grinnel, 145.

57 Bain, 290.

58 Ibid, 291.

59 Seymour, 83.

60 Ibid, 85.

61 Ibid, 86.

62 Ibid, 89.

63 Brey.

64 Seymour, 91.

65 Ibid, 94.

66 Bain, 293.

67 Seymour, 104.

68 Brey.

69 Seymour, 105.

70 Ibid, 107.

71 Ferguson diary, September 9, 1866.

72 Seymour, 124.

73 Bain, 345

74 Ibid.

75 Shearer, 41.

76 Bratt, 61-62.

77 Miller, Photog. of the Early West, 36.

78 Ibid, 107.

79 Andreas.

80 Ferguson diary, November 13, 1866.

81 Ferguson diary, November 14, 1866.

82 Lee, 60.

83 Nielsen, 12.

84 Shearer, 47.

85 Stansbery, 6.

86 Williams, Dallas, 2.

87 O'Dell, 50.

88 Scott, 87.

89 Ibid, 97.

90 O'Dell, 51.

91 Scott, 111.

92 Williams, Dallas, 5.

93 Dunn, Indian Vengeance, 2.

94 Williams, Dallas, 8.

95 Ibid, 15.

96 Ibid, 20.

97 Bain, 349.

98 Williams, Dallas, 46.

99 Lent, 165.

100 Ferguson diary, June 17, 1867.

101 Ibid, June 16, July 7, 1867

102 Ferguson diary , May 18, 1867.

103 Ibid, June 17, 1867.

104 Wolff, 7.

105 Ambrose, 344.

106 Ibid, 216.

CPSIA information can be obtained at www.ICGtesting.com
Printed in the USA
LVOW100939020713

341158LV00002B/82/P